cooking school

Chinese

cooking school
Chinese

Bring the flavors of China to life in your own kitchen!

Love Food ® is an imprint of Parragon Books Ltd

Parragon
Queen Street House
4 Queen Street
Bath BA1 1HE, UK

Copyright © Parragon Books Ltd 2009

Love Food ® and the accompanying heart device is a trademark of Parragon Books Ltd

ISBN: 978-1-4075-6262-9

Printed in China

Design by Pink Creative
Internal photography by Charlie Richards*
Internal food styling by Anna Burges-Lumsden
Internal prop styling by Sarah Waller
Front cover photography by Clive Streeter
Introduction by Christine McFadden

Notes for the Reader
This book uses imperial, metric, and US cup measurements. Follow the same units of measurement throughout; do not mix imperial and metric. All spoon measurements are level: teaspoons are assumed to be 5 ml, and tablespoons are assumed to be 15 ml. Unless otherwise stated, milk is assumed to be whole, eggs and individual vegetables, such as potatoes, are medium, and pepper is freshly ground black pepper.

Recipes using raw or very lightly cooked eggs should be avoided by infants, the elderly, pregnant women, convalescents, and anyone with a chronic condition. Pregnant and breastfeeding women are advised to avoid eating peanuts and peanut products. People with nut allergies should be aware that some of the prepared ingredients used in the recipes in this book may contain nuts. Always check the packaging before use.

* except pages 16, 40, 48, 60, 63, 72, 76, 79, 83, 84, 88, 91, 92, 96, 103, 112, 115, 119, 120, 131, 136, 144, 159, 160, 168, 171 & 172

Contents

Introduction

Mastering the basics of Chinese cooking will give you a marvelous opportunity to explore not only the fabulous array of ingredients, the all-important preparation techniques, and the different cooking methods, but also to go deeper into the history, geography, and culture that lie behind Chinese regional cuisines. Armed with this knowledge, you will be amazed at the ease with which you can create an impressive range of dishes in your own kitchen, whether it's a multi-dish Chinese meal or a simple accompaniment to your normal menu.

Regional Cooking

China is as vast as the United States, spanning many degrees of latitude. It has radical variations in climate, ranging from year-round subarctic conditions in the north, to the sweltering tropics of the southern coastal regions. China's topography is equally extreme. From the Tibetan Plateau in the northwest (11,800 ft/3,600 m) the land descends in a series of steps to the fertile coastal plains in the east and south. It is this diversity of topography and climate that lie behind the intriguing variations of regional cooking.

Peking (Northern Cuisine)

The food in this region relies on staples, such as wheat, sorghum, millet, and soybeans. Wheat is a major crop, which means that noodles are the order of the day rather than rice. The food tends to be homely and robust, although the well-known Peking Duck is an exception. Hearty lamb dishes are popular, such as Lamb with Black Bean Sauce, reflecting the influence of Chinese Muslims who, for religious reasons, eat lamb instead of pork.

Canton (Southern Cuisine)

Cantonese cuisine offers an astonishing melting pot of culinary feasts and is renowned for top-notch seafood, fresh fruit and vegetables, stunning stir-fries, and dim sum to die for. Considered the gold standard of Chinese cuisine, Cantonese food is the best known in the Western world, thanks to the large numbers of Chinese who emigrated to Europe and the United States in the nineteenth century. Cantonese dishes, such as Sweet-and-Sour Pork and Sweet-and-Sour Spareribs, are well known the world over.

Because Canton was the first Chinese trading port, the region is greatly influenced by foreign contact. For example, broccoli and asparagus were introduced from abroad and were popular in Canton before being taken up elsewhere. Cooking with fruit and fruit-based sauces, as in Fruity Duck Stir-Fry, is also typical of the region. Seasonings are typically kept light, with limited use of soy sauce, in order to let the ingredients shine.

Shanghai (Eastern Cuisine)

Based around the Chang Delta, this fertile region produces both rice and wheat as well as an abundance of fruit and vegetables. Fresh fish comes not only from the sea but also from the numerous lakes and rivers that crisscross the land. Perhaps least known in the West, Shanghai cuisine is a mixture of styles, characterized by rich complex flavors and the lavish use of the rich soy sauce for which the Chang Delta is renowned. Sugar is also a key ingredient, especially in salty dishes in which it balances flavor without introducing obvious sweetness.

Sichuan (Western Cuisine)

Known in China as "the land of plenty," Sichuan enjoys rich, fertile soil, a warm climate, and copious rainfall. The region produces an enormous variety of fruit, vegetables, fungi, and fish, which are put to good use in richly flavored, heavily sauced dishes.

Sichuan cuisine has much more to offer than the hot and spicy dishes for which it is famous in the West. Although chiles and pepper are certainly used as "warming" foods to counteract the region's inherent dampness, these pungent seasonings are never used in a way that overwhelms other ingredients. Delicately flavored bamboo shoots and tofu feature in the cuisine, and in restaurants "cool" and "medium" dishes as well as "hot" ones are usually on the menu. The region is also noted for pickled or dry-salted vegetables.

Cooking and Eating Styles

For the Chinese, food and its supply have always been of vital concern; it is deeply appreciated and nothing is ever wasted. Regardless of the region, food is prepared, cooked, and served in accordance with the age-old Taoist principles of Yin and Yang, in which balance and contrast are key. Some of the ingredients and cooking methods may vary from one region to another, but basically all dishes are unmistakably "Chinese."

What distinguishes Chinese food is the emphasis on harmonious blending of color, texture, aroma, and flavor, both in a single dish and in the dishes that make up the meal. Of great importance is "fire control," as the Chinese call it; there are at least 40 different methods of heating food! Understanding basics, such as preheating a wok until almost red hot, will help you to achieve the necessary texture, whether crisp or soft, wet or dry, or slippery or crunchy.

Timing is equally important. If the heat is sufficiently high, food will cook quickly, but beginners tend to make the mistake of cooking food for too long over too low a heat.

Also important are the size and the shape of the prepared ingredient; this must be appropriate for a particular method of cooking. For example, food for quick stir-frying is cut into small, thin slices of uniform size, and never into large chunks. This is not only for appearance's sake, but also because ingredients of the same size and shape cook in the same amount of time.

Chinese Meals and Snacks

Day-to-day meals eaten at home are usually fairly simple, although made up of a variety of dishes. The meal is served all at once, in contrast to a formal banquet where dishes are served in a prescribed sequence. Unlike Western convention, dishes are never allocated to individual diners; everything on the table is shared. The Chinese do not usually finish a meal with a dessert, although sweet dishes might punctuate a full-scale banquet and fruit might be served at the end of a multicourse restaurant meal. Sweet dishes are usually eaten between meals as snacks.

Snacking and street food play a big part in Chinese culture. The Chinese love to buy all kinds of tasty snacks that are freshly cooked at roadside stalls, eating them on the run as they go about their daily life. In the evening, the sidewalks are filled with groups of families and friends cooking, selling, and sharing delicious food. Living in overcrowded conditions as many Chinese do, getting together in this way is an important and enjoyable part of social life.

Menu Planning

For a shared meal allow one dish per person. For example, if cooking for only two or three people, serve one main dish with a vegetable side dish and a rice or noodle dish, plus a soup if you like. For an informal meal for four to six people, serve four dishes plus soup and rice; for a formal dinner for the same number, allow six to eight dishes. When cooking for large numbers, always increase the number of dishes instead of the quantity of ingredients. That way, you'll have more variety of flavor, color, and texture.

Fundamental Techniques

Chopping

Cut the ingredients into small, equal-size pieces so that they cook in the same amount of time. Shredding vegetables thinly and slicing them diagonally increases the surface area in contact with the hot oil and speeds up cooking.

Stir-Frying

Success depends on the wok being very hot before you add the oil—hold your hand flat about 2¾ inches/7 cm above the bottom of the wok until you feel the heat. Before you begin, have all the ingredients measured and prepared. Using a long-handled ladle or long, wooden cooking chopsticks, constantly stir the ingredients so that they all come in contact with the hot oil and are evenly cooked.

Deep-Frying

Use enough oil to create a depth of about 2 inches/5 cm. Heat it over a medium–high heat until a faint haze appears. If the oil is not hot enough, the food will act like a sponge and become soggy and greasy. Cook in small batches to avoid overcrowding the pan—too much food will reduce the temperature of the oil and lead to unevenly cooked food. Remove the food with a wire ladle or tongs and drain thoroughly on paper towels.

Steaming

Dependent on fresh ingredients, steaming is routinely used in China to cook a wide range of food, including whole fish, dumplings, vegetables, and morsels of poultry and meat. The food is placed on a plate or in a bamboo steamer above boiling liquid in the bottom of a wok and covered with a lid to trap the steam, which then permeates the food. Depending on size and density, food may be steamed for 10 minutes or up to 3 hours. Ingredients must be fresh to benefit from this technique.

Braising and Red Cooking

Braising is generally used for tougher cuts of meat and vegetables with dense flesh. The ingredients are briefly stir-fried, then simmered in stock until tender. Red cooking is a similar technique in which food is slowly braised in a rich, reddish brown sauce; soy sauce and sugar are key ingredients. Once cooked, the food takes on the color of the sauce and becomes meltingly tender.

Cooking Equipment

Chinese cooking tools and utensils have been used for thousands of years and, as such, have proved their worth. Although Western equivalents do an adequate job, a cleaver and a wok will make life easier when preparing and cooking Chinese food.

Cleaver

Equally useful for demolishing bones or chopping delicate herbs, the rectangular blade of the cleaver is wide, thick, and rigid and tapers down to a razor-sharp edge. It is handy for transferring ingredients from cutting board to wok. Once you become adept, you will be able to use a cleaver to slice, dice, fillet, shred, crush, and chop all kinds of food.

Wok

Traditionally made of iron, the wok conducts heat quickly and evenly—essential in Chinese cooking. During stir-frying, the conical shape tips the food back to the center, where the heat is most intense. If fitted with a lid and a stand for stability, a wok can also be used for steaming, braising, and simmering.

Steamer

The traditional Chinese bamboo steamer has gaps in the bamboo that allow excess moisture to escape, preventing the food from becoming waterlogged. Bamboo steamers come in a range of sizes and can be stacked in a wok or pan of boiling water, letting you cook several dishes at the same time.

Ladle

The Chinese use a special ladle for stir-frying. It has a wide, shallow bowl, which is ideal for lifting, tossing, and turning, and an extra-long handle that lets you keep at a distance from the heat. There are also wire mesh ladles that do an efficient job of scooping up deep-fried foods. The wire lets oil drain away quickly.

Ingredients

Before you start cooking Chinese food, you will need some basic seasonings, oils, and pantry items, many of which you are already likely to have. Most are easily found in supermarkets, health food stores, and Chinese grocers; more obscure items are available by mail order or on-line through the internet. The following basics will get you off to a good start.

ALCOHOLS FOR FLAVORING
Dry sherry or rice wine

NOODLES
Dried egg noodles
Dried rice noodles

NUTS AND SEEDS
Almonds
Cashews
Peanuts
Sesame seeds

OILS
Chili oil and sesame oil for seasoning
Vegetable oil or peanut oil for stir-frying and deep-frying

RICE
White long-grain

SAUCES
Bean sauce, black and yellow
Chili bean sauce
Hoisin sauce
Oyster sauce
Plum sauce
Soy sauce: Use light soy sauce for stir-fries and dark soy sauce for marinades and red cooking

SPICES
Cinnamon sticks
Dried chile flakes
Fennel seeds
Five-spice powder
Ground ginger
Star anise
Sichuan pepper

TOFU (BEAN CURD)
Both firm and soft varieties are useful

VEGETABLES, CANNED OR IN POUCHES
Baby corn
Bamboo shoots
Salted black beans
Straw mushrooms
Water chestnuts

VEGETABLES, DRIED
Dried Chinese mushrooms

VINEGARS
White rice vinegar for rice dishes
Brown rice vinegar for marinades and glazes
Black rice vinegar for slow-cooked stews

Meat and Poultry Dishes

China has countless meat and poultry dishes that are cooked in every imaginable way. Pork is the most widely eaten, with poultry coming a close second. Both are versatile, uniformly tender, and well suited to Chinese cooking methods. There are fewer beef dishes, partly for economic reasons, but also because beef is not as versatile as other meats—only tender cuts are suitable for stir-frying but these dry out during slow-cooking. Ground beef is common in Sichuan cuisine— Ants Climbing a Tree is a classic dish. Lamb is popular in northern China, where religious laws forbid the eating of pork.

Poultry plays an important symbolic role as well as a culinary one. The cock represents positiveness and aggression; the duck, happiness and fidelity; and the pigeon, filial concern and longevity. Turkey sometimes

shows up in Cantonese cooking, but it is not widely eaten in the rest of China because cooks consider it too large to be practical and the flesh can sometimes be dry and tough. In China, poultry is always purchased live, guaranteeing freshness. Obviously, keeping live fowl is not possible—or even desirable—for most Western cooks, but you should buy the best quality you can afford.

Although there are classic meat and poultry dishes throughout China, many of them vary, depending on the region. For example, Beef Chop Suey is a Cantonese classic, but Sichuan cooks spike it with pepper and northerners add plenty of garlic. Sweet-and-Sour Chicken is also typically Cantonese, but Gong Bau Chicken from Sichuan is a complex mix of flavors—hot and spicy as well as sweet and sour.

Wonton Soup

SERVES 6–8

WONTONS

6 oz/175 g ground pork, not too lean

8 oz/225 g shrimp, peeled, deveined, and chopped

½ tsp finely chopped fresh ginger

1 tbsp light soy sauce

1 tbsp Chinese rice wine

2 tsp finely chopped scallion

pinch of sugar

pinch of white pepper

dash of sesame oil

30 square wonton wrappers

1 egg white, lightly beaten

SOUP

8 cups chicken stock

2 tsp salt

½ tsp white pepper

2 tbsp finely chopped scallion

1 tbsp chopped cilantro leaves, to serve

1. For the wonton filling, mix together the pork, shrimp, ginger, soy sauce, rice wine, scallion, sugar, pepper, and sesame oil and stir well until the texture is thick and pasty. Set aside for at least 20 minutes.

2. To make the wontons, place a teaspoon of the filling at the center of a wrapper. Brush the edges with a little egg white. Bring the opposite points toward each other and press the edges together, creating a flowerlike shape. Repeat with the remaining wrappers and filling.

3. To make the soup, bring the stock to a boil and add the salt and pepper. Boil the wontons in the stock for about 5 minutes, or until the wrappers begin to wrinkle around the filling.

4. To serve, put the scallion in individual bowls, then spoon in the wontons and soup and sprinkle with the cilantro.

Ants Climbing a Tree

SERVES 4–6

4 oz/115 g ground pork
4 oz/115 g ground beef
3 tsp light soy sauce
pinch of salt
1 tbsp vegetable or peanut oil
1 tbsp chili bean paste

1 tsp dark soy sauce
¾ cup hot chicken stock
5 oz/140 g thin rice noodles, soaked in warm
    water for 20 minutes and drained
2 scallions, finely chopped

1. Combine the ground meats with 1 teaspoon of the light soy sauce and the salt.

2. In a preheated wok or deep pan, heat the oil and cook the ground meats until they begin to brown.
   Add the chili bean paste and stir rapidly. Stir in the dark soy sauce.

3. Pour in the stock, noodles, and remaining light soy sauce. Cover the wok or pan and simmer
   for about 8–10 minutes, or until the pan is dry. Shake the pan but do not stir. Toss in the scallions
   and serve.

Hoisin Pork with Garlic Noodles

SERVES 4

9 oz/250 g thick egg noodles or
   whole-wheat egg noodles

1 lb/450 g pork tenderloin, thinly sliced

1 tsp sugar

1 tbsp peanut or corn oil

4 tbsp rice vinegar

4 tbsp white wine vinegar

4 tbsp hoisin sauce

2 scallions, sliced diagonally

about 2 tbsp garlic-flavored oil

2 large garlic cloves, thinly sliced

chopped fresh cilantro, to garnish

1. Cook the noodles in a pan of boiling water for 3 minutes or according to the directions on the package. Drain well, rinse under cold water to stop the cooking, and drain again, then set aside.

2. Meanwhile, sprinkle the pork with the sugar and use your hands to toss together. Heat a wok over high heat. Add the peanut oil and heat until it shimmers. Add the pork and stir-fry for about 3 minutes, until the pork is cooked through and is no longer pink. Use a slotted spoon to remove the pork from the wok and keep warm. Add both vinegars to the wok and boil until they are reduced by about one third. Pour in the hoisin sauce with the scallions and let simmer until reduced by half. Add to the pork and stir together.

3. Quickly wipe out the wok and reheat. Add the garlic-flavored oil and heat until it shimmers. Add the garlic slices and stir around for about 30 seconds, until they are golden and crisp, then use a slotted spoon to scoop them out of the wok and set aside.

4. Add the noodles to the wok and stir them around to warm them through. Divide the noodles among 4 plates, top with the pork-and-scallion mixture, and sprinkle over the garlic slices and cilantro.

Pork Lo Mein

SERVES 4–6

6 oz/175 g boneless lean pork, shredded
8 oz/225 g egg noodles
1½ tbsp vegetable or peanut oil
2 tsp finely chopped garlic
1 tsp finely chopped fresh ginger
1 carrot, julienned
4 cups finely sliced shiitake mushrooms
1 green bell pepper, seeded and thinly sliced
1 tsp salt
½ cup hot chicken stock
1⅓ cups bean sprouts
2 tbsp finely chopped scallion

MARINADE
1 tsp light soy sauce
dash of sesame oil
pinch of white pepper

1. Combine all the marinade ingredients in a bowl and marinate the pork for at least 20 minutes.

2. Cook the noodles in a pan of boiling water for 4–5 minutes, or according to the directions on the package. When cooked, drain and set aside.

3. In a preheated wok or deep pan, heat ½ tablespoon of the oil and stir-fry the pork until the color has changed. Remove and set aside.

4. Quickly wipe out the wok and reheat. Add the remaining oil and stir-fry the garlic and ginger until fragrant. Add the carrot and cook for 1 minute, then add the mushrooms and cook for 1 minute. Toss in the bell pepper and cook for 1 minute. Add the pork, salt, and stock and heat through. Finally, toss in the noodles, followed by the bean sprouts, and stir well. Sprinkle with the scallion and serve.

Fried Rice with Pork and Shrimp

SERVES 4

3 tsp vegetable or peanut oil

1 egg, lightly beaten

3½ oz/100 g shrimp, peeled, deveined, and cut in half

3½ oz/100 g char siu or smoked bacon, finely chopped

2 tbsp finely chopped scallion

3 cups cooked rice, chilled

1 tsp salt

1. In a preheated wok or deep pan, heat 1 teaspoon of the oil and pour in the egg. Cook until scrambled. Remove and set aside.

2. Add the remaining oil and stir-fry the shrimp, cha siu, and scallion for about 2 minutes. Add the rice and salt, breaking up the rice into grains, and cook for an additional 2 minutes. Finally, stir in the cooked egg. Serve immediately.

Sweet-and-Sour Pork

SERVES 4

⅔ cup vegetable oil, for deep-frying

8 oz/225 g pork tenderloin, cut into
  ½-inch/1-cm cubes

1 onion, sliced

1 green bell pepper, seeded and sliced

8 oz/225 g canned pineapple chunks

1 small carrot, cut into thin strips

1 oz/25 g canned bamboo shoots, drained,
  rinsed, and halved

cooked rice, to serve

BATTER

scant ¾ cup all-purpose flour

1 tbsp cornstarch

1½ tsp baking powder

1 tbsp vegetable oil

SAUCE

⅔ cup light brown sugar

2 tbsp cornstarch

½ cup white wine vinegar

2 garlic cloves, crushed

4 tbsp tomato paste

6 tbsp pineapple juice

1. To make the batter, sift the flour into a mixing bowl, together with the cornstarch and baking powder. Add the oil and stir in enough water to make a thick, smooth batter (about ¾ cup).

2. Heat enough oil for deep-frying in a wok, deep-fat fryer, or large, heavy-bottom pan to 350–375°F/ 180–190°C, or until a cube of bread browns in 30 seconds.

3. Dip the cubes of pork into the batter and cook in the hot oil, in batches, until the pork is cooked through. Remove the pork from the wok with a slotted spoon and drain on paper towels. Set aside and keep the pork pieces warm until they are needed.

4. Drain all but 1 tablespoon of oil from the wok and return it to the heat. Add the onion, bell pepper, pineapple chunks, carrot, and bamboo shoots and cook for 1–2 minutes. Remove from the wok with a slotted spoon and set aside.

5. Mix all of the sauce ingredients together and pour into the wok. Bring to a boil, stirring until thickened and clear. Cook for 1 minute, then return the pork and vegetables to the wok. Cook for an additional 1–2 minutes, then transfer to a serving plate and serve with rice.

Soft-Wrapped Pork and Shrimp Rolls

MAKES 20

4 oz/115 g firm tofu, drained

3 tbsp vegetable or peanut oil

1 tsp finely chopped garlic

2 oz/55 g lean pork, shredded

4 oz/115 g shrimp, peeled and deveined

½ small carrot, cut into short, thin sticks

½ cup fresh or canned bamboo shoots, rinsed and shredded (if using fresh shoots, boil in water first for 30 minutes)

1 cup finely sliced cabbage

½ cup snow peas, julienned

1-egg omelet, shredded

1 tsp salt

1 tsp light soy sauce

1 tsp Chinese rice wine

pinch of white pepper

20 soft egg roll wrappers

chili bean sauce, to serve

1. Cut the tofu horizontally into thin slices. Heat 1 tablespoon of the oil in a wok and cook the tofu until it turns golden brown. Cut into thin strips and set aside.

2. In a preheated wok or deep pan, heat the remaining oil and stir-fry the garlic until fragrant. Add the pork and stir for about 1 minute, then add the shrimp and stir for an additional minute. One by one, stirring well after each, add the carrot, bamboo shoots, cabbage, snow peas, tofu, and, finally, the shredded omelet. Season with the salt, light soy sauce, rice wine, and pepper. Stir for an additional minute, then turn into a bowl.

3. To assemble each roll, smear an egg roll wrapper with a little chili bean sauce and place a heaped teaspoon of the filling toward the bottom of the circle. Roll up the bottom edge to secure the filling, turn in the sides, and continue to roll up gently. Cut each roll diagonally in half and arrange, cut-sides up, on a serving plate.

Pork and Ginger Dumplings

MAKES 50

1 lb/450 g ground pork, not too lean

1 tbsp light soy sauce

1½ tsp salt

1 tsp Chinese rice wine

½ tsp sesame oil

scant 1 cup very finely chopped cabbage

2 tsp minced fresh ginger

2 tsp finely chopped scallion

½ tsp white pepper

50 round wonton wrappers, about
   2¾ inches/7 cm in diameter

flour, for dusting

peanut oil, for oiling

DIPPING SAUCE

1 tbsp dark soy sauce

1 tbsp rice vinegar

½ tsp sugar

1 tsp chopped fresh ginger

1 tsp chopped garlic

1 fresh Thai red chile, seeded and finely
   chopped

1. To make the dipping sauce, stir all the ingredients together in a small bowl and set aside.

2. For the filling, mix the pork with the light soy sauce and ½ teaspoon of the salt. Stir carefully, always in the same direction, to create a thick paste. Add the rice wine and sesame oil and continue mixing in the same direction. Cover and let rest for at least 20 minutes.

3. To prepare the cabbage, sprinkle the fine shreds with the remaining salt to help draw out the water. Add the ginger, scallion, and white pepper and knead for at least 5 minutes into a thick paste. Combine with the pork mixture.

4. Place about 1 tablespoon of the filling in the center of each wrapper, holding the skin in the palm of one hand. Moisten the edges with water, then seal the edges with 2–3 pleats on each side and place on a lightly floured board.

5. Line a bamboo steamer with a circle of lightly oiled wax paper and replace the lid. Fill the base of the wok with enough water for steaming and place the bamboo steamer on top. Place over medium–high heat and bring to a boil. Transfer the dumplings, in batches, to the steamer, re-cover, and steam for 8–10 minutes, until cooked through. Using a slotted spoon, carefully transfer the dumplings to a serving plate.

6. Pour the dipping sauce into individual bowls, then serve with the dumplings.

Sweet-and-Sour Spareribs

SERVES 4

1 lb/450 g spareribs, cut into bite-size pieces

1½ tbsp vegetable or peanut oil, plus extra for deep-frying

1 green bell pepper, seeded and cut into 1-inch/2.5-cm chunks

1 small onion, coarsely chopped

1 small carrot, finely sliced

½ tsp finely chopped garlic

½ tsp finely chopped fresh ginger

3½ oz/100 g canned pineapple chunks

MARINADE

2 tsp light soy sauce

½ tsp salt

pinch of white pepper

SAUCE

3 tbsp white rice vinegar

2 tbsp sugar

1 tbsp light soy sauce

1 tbsp ketchup

1. Combine the marinade ingredients in a bowl with the spareribs and let marinate for at least 20 minutes.

2. Heat enough oil for deep-frying in a wok, deep-fat fryer, or large, heavy-bottom pan to 350–375°F/ 180–190°C, or until a cube of bread browns in 30 seconds. Deep-fry the spareribs for 8 minutes. Drain and set aside.

3. To make the sauce, mix together the vinegar, sugar, soy sauce, and ketchup. Set aside.

4. In a preheated wok, heat 1 tablespoon of the oil and stir-fry the bell pepper, onion, and carrot for 2 minutes. Remove and set aside.

5. Quickly wipe out the wok and reheat. Add the remaining oil and stir-fry the garlic and ginger until fragrant. Add the sauce, then bring back to a boil and add the pineapple chunks. Finally, add the spareribs and the bell pepper, onion, and carrot. Stir until warmed through and serve immediately.

Pork and Crab Meatballs

SERVES 6

8 oz/225 g pork tenderloin, finely chopped
5¾ oz/170 g canned crabmeat, drained
3 scallions, finely chopped
1 garlic clove, finely chopped
1 tsp Thai red curry paste
1 tbsp cornstarch
1 egg white
vegetable or peanut oil, for deep-frying
cooked rice, to serve

SAUCE
1 tbsp vegetable or peanut oil
2 shallots, chopped
1 garlic clove, crushed
2 large fresh red chiles, seeded and chopped
4 scallions, chopped
3 tomatoes, coarsely chopped

1. Put the pork and crabmeat into a bowl and mix together. Add the scallions, garlic, curry paste, cornstarch, and egg white and beat well to make a thick paste. With damp hands, shape the mixture into walnut-size balls.

2. Heat enough oil for deep-frying in a wok, deep-fat fryer, or large, heavy-bottom pan to 350–375°F/ 180–190°C, or until a cube of bread browns in 30 seconds. Deep-fry the balls, in batches, for 3–4 minutes, turning frequently, until golden brown and cooked. Drain on paper towels and keep warm.

3. To make the sauce, heat the oil in a wok and stir-fry the shallots and garlic for 1–2 minutes. Add the chiles and scallions and stir-fry for 1–2 minutes, then add the tomatoes. Stir together quickly, then spoon the sauce over the pork-and-crab balls. Serve immediately with rice.

Stir-Fried Lamb with Orange

SERVES 4

1 lb/450 g ground lamb

2 garlic cloves, crushed

1 tsp cumin seeds

1 tsp ground coriander

1 red onion, sliced

finely grated rind and juice of 1 orange

2 tbsp light soy sauce

1 orange, peeled and segmented

salt and pepper

snipped fresh chives and strips of orange zest, to garnish

1. Heat a wok or large skillet, without adding any oil. Add the ground lamb to the wok. Dry-fry the ground lamb for 5 minutes, or until the meat is evenly browned. Drain away any excess fat from the wok.

2. Add the garlic, cumin seeds, coriander, and red onion to the wok and cook for an additional 5 minutes.

3. Stir in the orange rind and juice and the soy sauce, mixing until thoroughly combined. Cover, reduce the heat, and let simmer, stirring occasionally, for 15 minutes.

4. Remove the lid, increase the heat, and add the orange segments. Stir to mix.

5. Season with salt and pepper to taste and heat through for an additional 2–3 minutes. Transfer the stir-fry to warmed serving plates and garnish with snipped fresh chives and strips of orange zest. Serve immediately.

Lamb with Black Bean Sauce

SERVES 4

1 lb/450 g lamb neck fillet or boneless
   leg of lamb

1 egg white, lightly beaten

4 tbsp cornstarch

1 tsp Chinese five-spice powder

3 tbsp sunflower oil

1 red onion, sliced

1 red bell pepper, seeded and sliced

1 green bell pepper, seeded and sliced

1 yellow or orange bell pepper,
   seeded and sliced

5 tbsp black bean sauce

cooked noodles, to serve

1. Using a sharp knife, slice the lamb into thin strips.

2. Mix together the egg white, cornstarch, and Chinese five-spice powder. Toss the lamb strips in the mixture until evenly coated.

3. Heat the oil in a wok and cook the lamb over high heat for 5 minutes, or until it crispens around the edges.

4. Add the onion and bell peppers to the wok and cook for 5–6 minutes, or until the vegetables just begin to soften.

5. Stir the black bean sauce into the mixture in the wok and heat through.

6. Transfer to warmed serving dishes and serve hot with noodles.

Beef Chop Suey

SERVES 4

1 lb/450 g rib-eye or sirloin steak, finely sliced

1 head of broccoli, cut into small florets

2 tbsp vegetable or peanut oil

1 onion, finely sliced

2 celery stalks, finely sliced diagonally

2 cups snow peas, sliced in half lengthwise

½ cup fresh or canned bamboo shoots, rinsed and julienned (if using fresh shoots, boil in water first for 30 minutes)

8 water chestnuts, finely sliced

4 cups finely sliced mushrooms

1 tbsp oyster sauce

1 tsp salt

MARINADE

1 tbsp Chinese rice wine

pinch of white pepper

pinch of salt

1 tbsp light soy sauce

½ tsp sesame oil

1. Combine all the marinade ingredients in a bowl and marinate the beef for at least 20 minutes. Blanch the broccoli in a large pan of boiling water for 30 seconds. Drain and set aside.

2. In a preheated wok or deep pan, heat 1 tablespoon of the oil and stir-fry the beef until the color has changed. Remove and set aside.

3. In the clean wok or deep pan, heat the remaining oil and stir-fry the onion for 1 minute. Add the celery and broccoli and cook for 2 minutes. Add the snow peas, bamboo shoots, water chestnuts, and mushrooms and cook for 1 minute. Add the beef, then season with the oyster sauce and salt and serve.

Beef Chow Mein

SERVES 4

10 oz/280 g beef tenderloin, cut into slivers
8 oz/225 g egg noodles
2 tbsp vegetable or peanut oil
1 onion, finely sliced
1 green bell pepper, finely sliced
1 cup bean sprouts
1 tsp salt
pinch of sugar
2 tsp Chinese rice wine
2 tbsp light soy sauce
1 tbsp dark soy sauce
1 tbsp finely shredded scallion

MARINADE
1 tsp light soy sauce
dash of sesame oil
½ tsp Chinese rice wine
pinch of white pepper

1. Combine all the marinade ingredients in a bowl and marinate the beef for at least 20 minutes.

2. Cook the noodles in a pan of boiling water for 4–5 minutes, or according to the directions on the package. When cooked, rinse under cold water and set aside.

3. In a preheated wok or deep pan, heat the oil and stir-fry the beef for about 1 minute, or until it has changed color. Stir in the onion and cook for 1 minute, then add the bell pepper and bean sprouts. Cook until any water from the vegetables has evaporated. Add the salt, sugar, rice wine, and soy sauces. Stir in the noodles and toss for 1 minute. Finally, stir in the scallion and serve.

Sweet-and-Sour Chicken

SERVES 4–6

1 lb/450 g lean chicken, cubed

5 tbsp vegetable or peanut oil

½ tsp minced garlic

½ tsp finely chopped fresh ginger

1 green bell pepper, seeded and cut into 1-inch/2.5-cm chunks

1 onion, coarsely chopped

1 carrot, finely sliced

1 tsp sesame oil

1 tbsp finely chopped scallion

cooked rice, to serve

MARINADE

2 tsp light soy sauce

1 tsp Chinese rice wine

pinch of white pepper

½ tsp salt

dash of sesame oil

SAUCE

8 tbsp rice vinegar

4 tbsp sugar

2 tsp light soy sauce

6 tbsp ketchup

1. Combine all the marinade ingredients in a bowl and marinate the chicken for at least 20 minutes.

2. To make the sauce, heat the vinegar in a pan and add the sugar, light soy sauce, and ketchup. Stir to dissolve the sugar, then set aside.

3. In a preheated wok, heat 3 tablespoons of the oil and stir-fry the chicken until it starts to turn golden brown. Remove and set aside. Wipe the wok clean.

4. In the clean wok, heat the remaining oil and cook the garlic and ginger until fragrant. Add the vegetables and cook for 2 minutes. Add the chicken and cook for 1 minute. Finally, add the sauce and sesame oil, then stir in the scallion and serve with rice.

Gong Bau Chicken

SERVES 4

2 boneless chicken breasts, with or without
  skin, cut into ½-inch/1-cm cubes
1 tbsp vegetable or peanut oil
10 dried red chiles or more, to taste, snipped
  into 2–3 pieces
1 tsp Sichuan peppers
3 garlic cloves, finely sliced
1-inch/2.5-cm piece fresh ginger, finely sliced
1 tbsp coarsely chopped scallion,
  white part only
generous ½ cup peanuts, roasted
cooked rice, to serve

MARINADE
2 tsp light soy sauce
1 tsp Chinese rice wine
½ tsp sugar

SAUCE
1 tsp light soy sauce
1 tsp dark soy sauce
1 tsp black Chinese rice vinegar
a few drops of sesame oil
2 tbsp chicken stock
1 tsp sugar

1. Combine all the marinade ingredients in a bowl and marinate the chicken, covered, for at least 20 minutes. Combine all the sauce ingredients in a separate bowl and set aside.

2. In a preheated wok, heat the oil and stir-fry the chiles and peppers until crisp and fragrant. Toss in the chicken pieces. When they begin to color, add the garlic, ginger, and scallion. Stir-fry for about 5 minutes, or until the chicken is cooked.

3. Pour in the sauce, mix together thoroughly, then stir in the peanuts. Serve immediately with rice.

Chicken and Shiitake Mushrooms

SERVES 4

2 tbsp vegetable oil

1 lb 8 oz/675 g chicken breast, skinned and
  cut into 1-inch/2.5-cm chunks

1 tsp grated fresh ginger

3 carrots, thinly sliced

2 onions, thinly sliced

¾ cup bean sprouts

4½ cups fresh or dried shiitake mushrooms,
  thinly sliced

3 tbsp chopped fresh cilantro

cooked rice noodles, to serve

SAUCE

scant 1 cup granulated sugar

1 cup light soy sauce

1 tsp Chinese five-spice powder

1 cup sweet sherry

1. To make the sauce, combine the sugar, soy sauce, Chinese five-spice powder, and sherry in a bowl.
   Mix well and set aside.

2. In a wok or skillet, heat the oil over medium–high heat. Add the chicken and stir-fry for 2 minutes,
   then add the ginger and cook for 1 minute, stirring continuously. Add the sauce and cook for an
   additional 2 minutes.

3. One at a time, add the carrots, onions, bean sprouts, mushrooms, and cilantro, stirring between
   each addition.

4. Once the sauce has reduced and is thick, transfer the stir-fry to warmed serving bowls. Serve
   immediately with noodles.

Cross-the-Bridge Noodles

SERVES 4

10½ oz/300 g thin egg or rice noodles
7 oz/200 g choy sum or similar green vegetable
8 cups chicken stock
½-inch/1-cm piece fresh ginger
1–2 tsp salt
1 tsp sugar

1 boneless, skinless chicken breast,
  finely sliced diagonally
7 oz/200 g whitefish fillet,
  finely sliced diagonally
1 tbsp light soy sauce

1. Cook the noodles according to the directions on the package. When cooked, rinse under cold water and set aside. Blanch the choy sum in a large pan of boiling water for 30 seconds. Rinse under cold water and set aside.

2. In a large pan, bring the stock to a boil, then add the ginger, salt, and sugar and skim the surface. Add the chicken and cook for about 4 minutes, then add the fish and simmer for an additional 4 minutes, or until the fish and chicken are cooked through.

3. Add the noodles and choy sum with the light soy sauce and bring back to a boil. Spoon into serving bowls and serve immediately.

Chicken with Cashew Nuts

SERVES 4–6

1 lb/450 g skinless, boneless chicken breast, cut into bite-size pieces

3 tbsp light soy sauce

1 tsp Chinese rice wine

pinch of sugar

½ tsp salt

3 dried Chinese mushrooms, soaked in warm water for 20 minutes

2 tbsp vegetable or peanut oil

4 slices of fresh ginger

1 tsp finely chopped garlic

1 red bell pepper, seeded and cut into 1-inch/2.5-cm chunks

generous ½ cup cashew nuts, roasted

1. Marinate the chicken in 2 tablespoons of the soy sauce, the rice wine, sugar, and salt for at least 20 minutes.

2. Squeeze any excess water from the mushrooms and finely slice, discarding any tough stems. Reserve the soaking water.

3. In a preheated wok, heat 1 tablespoon of the oil. Add the ginger and stir-fry until fragrant. Stir in the chicken and cook for 2 minutes, or until it begins to turn brown. Before the chicken is cooked through, remove and set aside. Wipe the wok clean.

4. In the clean wok, heat the remaining oil and stir-fry the garlic until fragrant. Add the mushrooms and bell pepper and stir-fry for 1 minute. Add about 2 tablespoons of the mushroom soaking water and cook for about 2 minutes, or until the water has evaporated.

5. Return the chicken to the wok, then add the remaining soy sauce and the cashew nuts and stir-fry for 2 minutes, or until the chicken is cooked through. Serve immediately.

Chicken Fried Rice

½ tbsp sesame oil
6 shallots, peeled and quartered
1 lb/450g cooked chicken, diced
3 tbsp light soy sauce
2 carrots, diced
1 celery stalk, diced

1 red bell pepper, seeded and diced
1½ cups fresh peas
3½ oz/100 g canned corn kernels, drained
4 cups cooked long-grain rice
2 large eggs, scrambled

1. Heat the oil in a large skillet over medium heat. Add the shallots and fry until softened, then add the chicken and 2 tablespoons of the soy sauce and stir-fry for 5–6 minutes.

2. Stir in the carrots, celery, bell pepper, peas, and corn and stir-fry for an additional 5 minutes. Add the rice and stir thoroughly.

3. Finally, stir in the scrambled eggs and the remaining soy sauce. Serve immediately.

Peking Duck

SERVES 6–10

1 duck, about 4 lb 8 oz/2 kg
7 cups boiling water
1 tbsp honey
1 tbsp Chinese rice wine
1 tsp white rice vinegar

TO SERVE
1 cucumber, seeded and julienned
10 scallions, white part only, shredded
30 Peking duck wrappers
plum or hoisin sauce

1. To prepare the duck, massage the skin to separate it from the meat.

2. Pour the boiling water into a large pan, then add the honey, rice wine, and vinegar and lower in the duck. Baste for about 1 minute. Remove the duck and hang it to dry for a few hours or overnight.

3. Preheat the oven to 400°F/200°C. Place the duck on a rack above a roasting pan and roast in the preheated oven for at least 1 hour, or until the skin is crispy and the duck is cooked through.

4. Bring the duck to the table, together with the cucumber, scallions, wrappers, and plum or hoisin sauce. First carve the skin off the duck, then carve the meat. Shred the skin and meat into bite-size strips. Place a little of the duck on a wrapper, top with some cucumber and scallions, and drizzle over a little of the sauce. Roll up the wrapper and repeat with the remaining ingredients. Serve immediately.

Fruity Duck Stir-Fry

SERVES 4

4 duck breasts
1 tsp Chinese five-spice powder
1 tbsp cornstarch
1 tbsp chili oil
8 oz/225 g pearl onions, peeled
2 garlic cloves, crushed

3½ oz/100 g baby corn
1¼ cups canned pineapple chunks, drained
6 scallions, sliced
1 cup bean sprouts
2 tbsp plum sauce

1. Remove any skin from the duck breasts. Cut the duck into thin slices.

2. Mix together the Chinese five-spice powder and cornstarch. Toss the duck in the mixture until well coated.

3. Heat the oil in a preheated wok. Cook the duck for 10 minutes, or until just beginning to crispen around the edges. Remove from the wok and set aside.

4. Add the onions and garlic to the wok and cook for 5 minutes, or until softened. Add the baby corn and cook for an additional 5 minutes. Add the pineapple, scallions, and bean sprouts and cook for 3–4 minutes. Stir in the plum sauce.

5. Return the cooked duck to the wok and toss until well mixed. Transfer to warmed serving dishes and serve hot.

Turkey, Broccoli, and Bok Choy

SERVES 4

1 lb/450 g turkey breast, cut into strips

1 tbsp vegetable oil

1 head of broccoli, cut into florets

2 heads of bok choy, leaves washed and
   separated (or savoy cabbage,
   if bok choy is unavailable)

1 red bell pepper, seeded and thinly sliced

¼ cup chicken stock

MARINADE

1 tbsp light soy sauce

1 tbsp honey

2 garlic cloves, crushed

1. To make the marinade, combine the soy sauce, honey, and garlic in a medium bowl. Add the turkey and toss to coat. Cover the bowl with plastic wrap and let marinate in the refrigerator for 2 hours.

2. Put a wok or large skillet over medium–high heat, add the oil, and heat for 1 minute. Add the turkey and stir-fry for 3 minutes, or until the turkey has changed color. Remove with a slotted spoon, then set aside and keep warm.

3. Add the broccoli, bok choy, and bell pepper to the wok and stir-fry for 2 minutes. Add the stock and continue to stir-fry for 2 minutes, or until the vegetables are crisp yet tender.

4. Return the turkey to the wok and stir-fry briefly to warm through. Serve immediately.

Turkey with Bamboo Shoots and Water Chestnuts

SERVES 4

1 lb/450 g turkey breast, cubed

1 tbsp sesame oil

10 small mushrooms, halved

1 green bell pepper, seeded and cut into strips

1 zucchini, halved and thinly sliced

4 scallions, quartered

4 oz/115 g canned bamboo shoots, drained

4 oz/115 g canned sliced water chestnuts, drained

MARINADE

4 tbsp sweet sherry

1 tbsp lemon juice

1 tbsp light soy sauce

2 tsp grated fresh ginger

1 garlic clove, crushed

1. To make the marinade, combine the sherry, lemon juice, soy sauce, ginger, and garlic in a bowl, then add the turkey and stir. Cover with plastic wrap and let marinate in the refrigerator for 3–4 hours.

2. In a wok or skillet, add the oil and heat. Remove the turkey from the marinade with a slotted spoon (reserving the marinade) and stir-fry a few pieces at a time until browned. Remove the turkey from the wok and set aside.

3. Add the mushrooms, bell pepper, and zucchini to the wok and stir-fry for 3 minutes. Add the scallions and stir-fry for an additional minute. Add the bamboo shoots and water chestnuts to the wok, then add the turkey along with half of the reserved marinade. Stir over medium–high heat for an additional 2–3 minutes, or until the ingredients are evenly coated and the marinade has reduced.

4. Serve immediately in warmed bowls.

Fish and Seafood Dishes

China's extensive coastline and inland waterways offer a huge variety of fresh- and saltwater fish and seafood. Favorites include pike, carp, Mandarin fish (a type of perch), shad, and grouper, plus many other varieties familiar in the West. Shrimp are widely consumed, and scallops, squid, and clams cooked in spicy sauces are also popular.

Somewhat surprisingly, freshwater fish and shellfish play a much bigger part in the Chinese diet than those from the sea, despite 3,000 miles/4,800 km of coastline. This is partly because much of it is farmed in special ponds that are restocked each year, but also because freshwater fish and shellfish, especially crabs and shrimp, are considered sweeter and more delicate than their saltwater equivalents. Soft-shell, freshwater crabs, in particular, are highly prized in Peking.

The Chinese like to cook their fish whole, either steamed, quickly poached, or deep-fried. Lobster and crab are sometimes fried in flavored oil that penetrates the cracked shells, creating a most delectable sauce that the Chinese love to suck from the shells.

Although fish and seafood are commonplace in the kitchen, the Chinese do not like fishy smells. Ginger, garlic, and salty black bean sauce are often used to disguise such smells. Freshness is paramount—no respectable cook would dream of buying anything but a live fish, purchased in a leak-proof basket and kept alive until just before cooking. While this is not usually possible in the West, it is advisable to purchase fish and seafood from a reputable fish supplier. Fresh fish should never smell fishy— this is a sign that it's past its best.

Seafood Chow Mein

SERVES 4

3 oz/85 g squid, cleaned

3–4 prepared scallops

3 oz/85 g shrimp, peeled and deveined

½ egg white, lightly beaten

2 tsp cornstarch, mixed to a paste with
    2½ tsp water

9½ oz/275 g egg noodles

5–6 tbsp vegetable oil

2 tbsp light soy sauce

2 oz/55 g snow peas

½ tsp salt

½ tsp sugar

1 tsp Chinese rice wine

2 scallions, finely shredded

a few drops of sesame oil

1. Open up the squid and score the inside in a crisscross pattern, then cut into bite-size pieces. Soak the squid in a bowl of boiling water until all the pieces curl up. Rinse in cold water and drain.

2. Cut each scallop into 3–4 slices. Cut the shrimp in half lengthwise if large. Mix the scallops and shrimp with the egg white and cornstarch paste.

3. Cook the noodles according to the directions on the package. Drain and rinse under cold water. Drain well, then toss with about 1 tablespoon of oil.

4. Heat 3 tablespoons of oil in a preheated wok. Add the noodles and 1 tablespoon of the soy sauce and stir-fry for 2–3 minutes. Transfer to a large serving dish.

5. Heat the remaining oil in the wok and add the snow peas and seafood. Stir-fry for about 2 minutes, then add the salt, sugar, rice wine, the remaining soy sauce, and about half the scallions. Mix well and add a little water if necessary. Pour the seafood mixture on top of the noodles and sprinkle with sesame oil. Garnish with the remaining scallions and serve.

Five-Willow Fish

SERVES 4–6

1 whole sea bass or similar, weighing
   1–1 lb 8 oz/450–675 g, gutted

2 tsp salt

6 tbsp vegetable or peanut oil

2 slices fresh ginger

2 garlic cloves, finely sliced

2 scallions, coarsely chopped

1 green bell pepper, seeded and thinly sliced

1 red bell pepper, seeded and thinly sliced

1 carrot, finely sliced

½ cup fresh or canned bamboo shoots, rinsed
   and thinly sliced (if using fresh shoots, boil in
   water first for 30 minutes)

2 tomatoes, peeled, seeded, and thinly sliced

1 tbsp Chinese rice wine

2 tbsp white rice vinegar

1 tbsp light soy sauce

1 tbsp sugar

1. Clean the fish and dry thoroughly. Score the fish on both sides with deep, diagonal cuts. Press ½ teaspoon of the salt into the skin.

2. In a preheated wok, heat 4 tablespoons of the oil and cook the fish for about 4 minutes on each side, or until cooked through. Drain, then set aside on a warmed dish and keep warm. Wipe the wok clean.

3. In the clean preheated wok, heat the remaining oil and stir-fry the ginger, garlic, and scallions until fragrant. Toss in the vegetables with the remaining salt and stir rapidly for 2–3 minutes. Add the remaining ingredients and mix well for 2–3 minutes. Pour the sauce over the fish and serve immediately.

Salmon and Scallops with Cilantro and Lime

SERVES 4

6 tbsp peanut oil

10 oz/280 g salmon steak, skinned and cut into 1-inch/2.5-cm chunks

8 oz/225 g prepared scallops

3 carrots, thinly sliced

2 celery stalks, cut into 1-inch/2.5-cm pieces

2 yellow bell peppers, seeded and thinly sliced

3 cups oyster mushrooms, thinly sliced

1 garlic clove, crushed

6 tbsp chopped fresh cilantro

3 shallots, thinly sliced

juice of 2 limes

1 tsp grated lime rind

1 tsp dried red pepper flakes

3 tbsp dry sherry

3 tbsp light soy sauce

1. In a large wok or skillet, heat the oil over medium heat. Add the salmon and scallops and stir-fry for 3 minutes. Remove from the wok, then set aside and keep warm.

2. Add the carrots, celery, bell peppers, mushrooms, and garlic to the wok and stir-fry for 3 minutes. Stir in the cilantro and shallots.

3. Add the lime juice and rind, dried red pepper flakes, sherry, and soy sauce and stir. Return the salmon and scallops to the wok and stir-fry carefully for an additional minute. Serve immediately.

Ginger-Marinated Salmon and Scallop Skewers

SERVES 4

RICE SALAD
7 oz/200 g brown basmati rice
½ cucumber, diced
4 scallions, sliced
½ bunch fresh cilantro, chopped
1 red bell pepper, seeded and diced
1 fresh green chile, seeded and thinly sliced
juice of 1 lime
2 tbsp sesame oil

SKEWERS
1 lb 2 oz/500 g salmon fillet, skinned and
   cut into chunks
8 prepared scallops
1½-inch/4-cm piece fresh ginger
juice of 1 lemon
1 tbsp olive oil

salad greens, to serve

1. Bring a large pan of water to a boil, add the rice, and cook for 25 minutes, or until tender. Drain and let cool. Mix the cooled rice with the cucumber, scallions, cilantro, bell pepper, chile, lime juice, and sesame oil in a bowl. Cover and set aside for the flavors to develop.

2. Meanwhile, put the salmon chunks and scallops into a shallow, nonmetallic bowl. Using a garlic press or the back of a knife, crush the ginger to extract the juice. Mix the ginger juice with the lemon juice and olive oil in a small bowl or pitcher and pour over the seafood. Turn the seafood to coat in the marinade. Cover and let marinate in the refrigerator for 30 minutes. Soak 8 wooden skewers in cold water for 30 minutes, then drain.

3. Preheat the broiler to high. Thread the salmon and scallops onto the skewers. Cook under the preheated broiler for 3–4 minutes on each side, or until cooked through.

4. Serve the hot seafood skewers with the rice salad and salad greens.

Monkfish Stir-Fry

SERVES 4

2 tsp sesame oil
1 lb/450 g monkfish fillets, cut into
    1-inch/2.5-cm chunks
1 onion, thinly sliced
3 garlic cloves, finely chopped
1 tsp grated fresh ginger

8 oz/225 g fine asparagus
3 cups thinly sliced mushrooms
2 tbsp light soy sauce
1 tbsp lemon juice

1. Heat the oil in a skillet over medium–high heat. Add the fish, onion, garlic, ginger, asparagus, and mushrooms. Stir-fry for 2–3 minutes.

2. Stir in the soy sauce and lemon juice and cook for an additional minute. Remove from the heat and transfer to warmed serving dishes. Serve immediately.

Fried Fish with Pine Nuts

SERVES 4–6

½ tsp salt

1 lb/450 g thick whitefish fillets, cut into
1-inch/2.5-cm cubes

2 dried Chinese mushrooms, soaked in warm
water for 20 minutes

3 tbsp vegetable or peanut oil

1-inch/2.5-cm piece fresh ginger,
finely shredded

1 tbsp chopped scallion

1 red bell pepper, seeded and cut into
1-inch/2.5-cm squares

1 green bell pepper, seeded and cut into
1-inch/2.5-cm squares

¼ cup fresh or canned bamboo shoots, rinsed
and cut into small cubes (if using fresh
shoots, boil in water first for 30 minutes)

2 tsp Chinese rice wine

2 tbsp pine nuts, toasted

cooked rice, to serve

1. Sprinkle the salt over the fish and set aside for 20 minutes. Squeeze out any excess water from the mushrooms and finely slice, discarding any tough stems.

2. In a preheated wok, heat 2 tablespoons of the oil and stir-fry the fish for 3 minutes. Drain the fish and set aside, then wipe the wok clean.

3. In the clean, preheated wok, heat the remaining oil and toss in the ginger. Stir until fragrant, then add the scallion, bell peppers, bamboo shoots, mushrooms, and rice wine and cook for 1–2 minutes.

4. Finally, add the fish and stir to warm through. Sprinkle with pine nuts and serve with rice.

Sweet-and-Sour Sea Bass

SERVES 2

scant 1 cup shredded bok choy

generous ¼ cup bean sprouts

generous ½ cup sliced shiitake mushrooms

generous ½ cup torn oyster mushrooms

scant ¼ cup finely sliced scallion

1 tsp finely grated fresh ginger

1 tbsp finely sliced lemongrass

2 skinless, boneless sea bass fillets,
    about 3¼ oz/90 g each

1 tbsp sesame seeds, toasted

SWEET-AND-SOUR SAUCE

⅓ cup pineapple juice

1 tbsp sugar

1 tbsp red wine vinegar

2 star anise, crushed

⅓ cup tomato juice

1 tbsp cornstarch, blended with a little
    cold water

1. Preheat the oven to 400°F/200°C. Cut 2 pieces of wax paper into 15-inch/38-cm squares and cut 2 pieces of aluminum foil to the same size.

2. To make the sauce, heat the pineapple juice, sugar, vinegar, star anise, and tomato juice in a pan, let simmer for 1–2 minutes, then thicken with the cornstarch paste, whisking constantly. Pour through a fine strainer into a small bowl and let cool.

3. In a separate large bowl, mix together the bok choy, bean sprouts, mushrooms, and scallion, then add the ginger and lemongrass. Toss all the ingredients together.

4. Put a square of wax paper on top of a square of foil and fold into a triangle. Open up and place half the vegetable mixture into the center, pour half the sauce over the vegetables, and place the sea bass on top. Sprinkle with a few sesame seeds. Close the triangle over the mixture and, starting at the top, fold the right corner and crumple the edges together to form an airtight triangular parcel. Repeat to make the second parcel.

5. Place onto a baking sheet and cook in the preheated oven for 10 minutes, until the foil parcels puff with steam. To serve, place on individual plates and snip the parcels open.

Deep-Fried River Fish with Chili Bean Sauce

SERVES 4–6

1 whole freshwater fish, such as trout or carp, weighing 14 oz/400 g, gutted
1 tbsp all-purpose flour
pinch of salt
scant ½ cup water
vegetable or peanut oil, for deep-frying

SAUCE
scant ½ cup vegetable or peanut oil
1 tsp dried chile flakes
1 garlic clove, finely chopped
1 tsp finely chopped fresh ginger
1 tbsp chili bean sauce
½ tsp white pepper
2 tsp sugar
1 tbsp white rice vinegar
1 tsp finely chopped scallion

1. To prepare the fish, clean and dry thoroughly. Mix together the flour, salt, and water to create a light batter. Use to coat the fish.

2. Heat enough oil for deep-frying in a wok, deep-fat fryer, or large, heavy-bottom pan to 350–375°F/ 180–190°C, or until a cube of bread browns in 30 seconds. Deep-fry the fish on one side at a time until the skin is crisp and golden brown. Drain, then set aside and keep warm.

3. To make the sauce, first heat all but 1 tablespoon of the oil in a small pan and, when smoking, pour over the chile flakes. Set aside.

4. In a preheated wok or deep pan, heat the remaining oil and stir-fry the garlic and ginger until fragrant. Stir in the chili bean sauce, then add the oil-and-chile flake mixture. Season with the pepper, sugar, and vinegar. Turn off the heat and stir in the scallion. Pour over the fish and serve immediately.

Wok-Fried Jumbo Shrimp in Spicy Sauce

SERVES 4

3 tbsp vegetable or peanut oil

1 lb/450 g jumbo shrimp, deveined but unpeeled

2 tsp finely chopped fresh ginger

1 tsp finely chopped garlic

1 tbsp chopped scallion

2 tbsp chili bean sauce

1 tsp Chinese rice wine

1 tsp sugar

½ tsp light soy sauce

1–2 tbsp chicken stock

1. In a preheated wok, heat the oil, then add in the shrimp and stir-fry over high heat for about 4 minutes. Arrange the shrimp on the sides of the wok out of the oil, then add in the ginger and garlic and stir until fragrant. Add the scallion and chili bean sauce. Stir the shrimp into this mixture.

2. Reduce the heat slightly and add the rice wine, sugar, soy sauce, and stock. Cover and cook for an additional minute. Serve immediately.

Ginger Shrimp with Oyster Mushrooms

SERVES 4

SAUCE
2/3 cup chicken stock
2 tsp sesame seeds
3 tsp grated fresh ginger
1 tbsp light soy sauce
1/4 tsp hot pepper sauce
1 tsp cornstarch

3–4 tbsp vegetable oil
3 carrots, thinly sliced
7 cups thinly sliced oyster mushrooms
1 large red bell pepper, seeded and
   thinly sliced
1 lb/450 g large shrimp, peeled and deveined
2 garlic cloves, crushed
fresh cilantro leaves, to garnish
cooked rice, to serve

1. To make the sauce, stir together the stock, sesame seeds, ginger, soy sauce, hot pepper sauce, and cornstarch in a small bowl until well blended. Set aside.

2. In a large wok or skillet, heat 2 tablespoons of the oil. Stir-fry the carrots for 3 minutes, then remove from the wok and set aside.

3. Add 1 tablespoon of the remaining oil to the wok and cook the mushrooms for 2 minutes. Remove from the wok and set aside.

4. Add the remaining oil to the wok, if needed, and stir-fry the bell pepper with the shrimp and garlic for 3 minutes, or until the shrimp turn pink and opaque.

5. Stir the sauce and pour it into the wok. Cook until the mixture bubbles, then return the carrots and mushrooms to the wok. Cover and cook for an additional 2 minutes, or until heated through.

6. Garnish with cilantro leaves and serve immediately with rice.

Shrimp Fu Yung

SERVES 4–6

1 tbsp vegetable or peanut oil
4 oz/115 g large shrimp, peeled and deveined
4 eggs, lightly beaten

1 tsp salt
pinch of white pepper
2 tbsp snipped Chinese chives

1. In a preheated wok, heat the oil and stir-fry the shrimp until they begin to turn pink.

2. Season the eggs with the salt and pepper and pour over the shrimp. Stir-fry for 1 minute, then add the chives.

3. Cook for an additional 4 minutes, stirring all the time, until the eggs are cooked through but still soft in texture. Serve immediately.

Drunken Shrimp

7 oz/200 g jumbo shrimp, peeled and deveined
1¼ cups Chinese rice wine
2 tbsp cognac

½ tsp salt
1 tbsp finely chopped scallion
1 tsp finely chopped fresh ginger

1. Blanch the shrimp in a large pan of boiling water for 30 seconds. Drain and set aside.

2. Combine all the ingredients, then cover and let stand at room temperature for about 1 hour. Strain and serve cold.

Chiles Stuffed with Fish Paste

SERVES 4–6

8 oz/225 g whitefish, ground

2 tbsp lightly beaten egg

4–6 large fresh red and green chiles

1 tbsp vegetable or peanut oil, plus extra for shallow-frying

2 garlic cloves, finely chopped

½ tsp fermented black beans, rinsed and lightly mashed

1 tbsp light soy sauce

pinch of sugar

1 tbsp water

MARINADE

1 tsp finely chopped fresh ginger

pinch of salt

pinch of white pepper

½ tsp vegetable or peanut oil

1. To make the marinade, combine all the ingredients in a bowl and marinate the fish for 20 minutes. Add the egg and mix by hand to create a smooth fish paste.

2. To prepare the chiles, cut in half lengthwise and scoop out the seeds and membranes. Cut into bite-size pieces. Spread each piece of chile with about ½ teaspoon of the fish paste.

3. In a preheated wok, heat enough oil for shallow-frying and cook the chile pieces on both sides, until they begin to turn golden brown. Drain the chiles, set aside, and wipe the wok clean.

4. Heat the 1 tablespoon of oil in the clean wok and stir-fry the garlic until aromatic. Stir in the black beans and mix well. Add the soy sauce and sugar and stir, then add the chile pieces. Add the water, then cover and simmer over a low heat for 5 minutes. Serve immediately.

Crispy Crab Wontons

MAKES 24

6 oz/175 g white crabmeat, drained if canned
  and thawed if frozen, flaked

1¾ oz/50 g canned water chestnuts, drained,
  rinsed, and chopped

1 small fresh red chile, chopped

1 scallion, chopped

1 tbsp cornstarch

1 tsp dry sherry

1 tsp light soy sauce

½ tsp lime juice

24 square wonton wrappers

vegetable oil, for deep-frying

fresh chives and lime slices, to garnish

1. To make the filling, mix the crabmeat, water chestnuts, chile, scallion, cornstarch, sherry, soy sauce, and lime juice together in a bowl.

2. Spread the wonton wrappers out on a counter and spoon an equal portion of the filling into the center of each wonton wrapper.

3. Dampen the edges of the wonton wrappers with a little water and fold them in half to form triangles. Fold the 2 bottom corners in toward the center, moisten with a little water to secure, then pinch together to seal.

4. Heat enough oil for deep-frying in a wok, deep-fat fryer, or large, heavy-bottom pan to 350–375°F/ 180–190°C, or until a cube of bread browns in 30 seconds. Deep-fry the wontons in batches for 2–3 minutes, until golden brown and crisp. Remove with a slotted spoon and drain on paper towels.

5. Serve the wontons hot, garnished with chives and lime slices.

Scallops in Black Bean Sauce

SERVES 4

2 tbsp vegetable or peanut oil

1 tsp finely chopped garlic

1 tsp finely chopped fresh ginger

1 tbsp fermented black beans, rinsed and lightly mashed

14 oz/400 g prepared scallops

½ tsp light soy sauce

1 tsp Chinese rice wine

1 tsp sugar

3–4 fresh red Thai chiles, finely chopped

1–2 tsp chicken stock

1 tbsp finely chopped scallion

1. Heat the oil in a preheated wok. Add the garlic and stir, then add the ginger and stir-fry together for about 1 minute, or until fragrant. Mix in the black beans, add the scallops, and stir-fry for 1 minute. Add the soy sauce, rice wine, sugar, and chiles.

2. Reduce the heat and simmer for 2 minutes, then add the stock. Finally, add the scallion, then stir and serve.

Baby Squid Stuffed with Pork and Mushrooms

SERVES 6–8

14 oz/400 g squid

4 dried Chinese mushrooms, soaked in warm
water for 20 minutes

8 oz/225 g ground pork

4 water chestnuts, finely chopped

½ tsp sesame oil

1 tsp salt

½ tsp white pepper

vegetable oil, for oiling

DIPPING SAUCE

4 tbsp dark soy sauce

1 fresh red Thai chile, chopped (optional)

1. Clean the squid thoroughly, removing all the tentacles. Squeeze out any excess water from the mushrooms and finely chop, discarding any tough stems.

2. Mix the mushrooms with the pork, water chestnuts, oil, salt, and pepper.

3. Force the stuffing into the squids, pressing firmly but leaving enough room to secure each one with a toothpick.

4. Line a bamboo steamer with a circle of lightly oiled wax paper and replace the lid. Fill the bottom of a wok with enough water for steaming and place the bamboo steamer on top. Place over medium–high heat and bring to a boil. Transfer the squid to the steamer, re-cover, and steam for 15 minutes, until cooked through.

5. Meanwhile, make the dipping sauce. Pour the soy sauce into a small serving bowl and mix in the chile, if using. Set aside.

6. Using a slotted spoon, carefully transfer the squid to a serving plate. Serve with the dipping sauce.

Stir-Fried Squid with Hot Black Bean Sauce

SERVES 4

1 lb 10 oz/750 g squid, cleaned and
  tentacles discarded
1 large red bell pepper, seeded
scant 1 cup snow peas
1 head of bok choy
1 tbsp corn oil
1 small fresh red Thai chile, chopped
1 garlic clove, finely chopped
1 tsp grated fresh ginger
2 scallions, chopped

SAUCE
3 tbsp black bean sauce
1 tbsp Thai fish sauce
1 tbsp rice wine or dry sherry
1 tbsp dark soy sauce
1 tsp brown sugar
1 tsp cornstarch
1 tbsp water

1. Cut the squid body cavities into quarters lengthwise. Use the tip of a small, sharp knife to score a diamond pattern into the flesh without cutting all the way through. Pat dry with paper towels.

2. Cut the bell pepper into long, thin slices. Cut the snow peas in half diagonally. Coarsely shred the bok choy.

3. To make the sauce, mix the black bean sauce, fish sauce, rice wine, soy sauce, and sugar together in a bowl. Blend the cornstarch with the water and stir into the other ingredients in the bowl. Reserve the mixture until required.

4. Heat the oil in a preheated wok. Add the chile, garlic, ginger, and scallions and stir-fry for 1 minute. Add the bell pepper slices and stir-fry for 2 minutes.

5. Add the squid and stir-fry over high heat for an additional minute. Stir in the snow peas and bok choy and stir for an additional minute, or until the bok choy has wilted.

6. Stir in the sauce ingredients and cook, stirring constantly, for 2 minutes, or until the sauce thickens and clears. Serve immediately on warmed plates.

Sweet Chile Squid

SERVES 4

2½ tbsp sesame oil
10 oz/280 g prepared squid, cut into strips
2 red bell peppers, seeded and thinly sliced
3 shallots, thinly sliced
1½ cups mushrooms, thinly sliced
1 tbsp dry sherry
4 tbsp light soy sauce

1 tsp sugar
1 tsp hot chile flakes, or to taste
1 garlic clove, crushed
1 tbsp sesame seeds, toasted
cooked rice, to serve

1. Heat 1 tablespoon of the oil in a skillet over medium heat. Add the squid and cook for 2 minutes. Remove from the skillet and set aside.

2. Add 1 tablespoon of the remaining oil to the skillet and cook the bell peppers and shallots over medium heat for 1 minute. Add the mushrooms and cook for an additional 2 minutes.

3. Return the squid to the skillet and add the sherry, soy sauce, sugar, chile flakes, and garlic, stirring thoroughly. Cook for another 2 minutes.

4. Sprinkle with the sesame seeds, then drizzle over the remaining oil and mix. Serve immediately with rice.

Stir-Fried Fresh Crab with Ginger

SERVES 4

3 tbsp vegetable or peanut oil

2 large fresh crabs, cleaned, broken into pieces, and legs cracked with a cleaver

1½-inch/4-cm piece fresh ginger, julienned

7 scallions, chopped into 2-inch/5-cm lengths

2 tbsp light soy sauce

1 tsp sugar

pinch of white pepper

1. In a preheated wok, heat 2 tablespoons of the oil and cook the crab over high heat for 3–4 minutes. Remove and set aside. Wipe the wok clean.

2. In the clean wok, heat the remaining oil, then add the ginger and stir until fragrant. Add the scallions, then stir in the crab pieces. Add the soy sauce, sugar, and pepper. Cover and simmer for 1 minute, then serve immediately in warmed bowls.

Clams in Black Bean Sauce

SERVES 4

2 lb/900 g small clams
1 tbsp vegetable or peanut oil
1 tsp finely chopped fresh ginger
1 tsp finely chopped garlic
1 tbsp fermented black beans, rinsed and
    coarsely chopped

2 tsp Chinese rice wine
1 tbsp finely chopped scallion
1 tsp salt (optional)

1. Discard any clams with broken shells and any that refuse to close when tapped. Wash the remaining clams thoroughly and let soak in clean water until ready to cook.

2. In a preheated wok, heat the oil and stir-fry the ginger and garlic until fragrant. Add the black beans and cook for 1 minute.

3. Over a high heat, add the clams and rice wine and stir-fry for 2 minutes to mix everything together. Cover and cook for about 3 minutes. Discard any clams that remain closed. Add the scallion and salt, if needed, and serve immediately.

Vegetable Dishes

Because of its vast size and varying climate, China produces an amazing variety of vegetables and the Chinese have perfected the art of cooking them. Cooks visit the market on a daily basis to make sure they get the freshest and best vegetables available; anything even slightly substandard will be firmly rejected.

Vegetables are integral to every meal and far more are consumed than meat or poultry. With few exceptions, meat and poultry dishes are always combined with some kind of vegetable, and soups often include slivers of colorful vegetables, such as bell peppers, boy choy, and carrots, and tasty flavorings, such as ginger and chiles. Stir-frying, in which ingredients are quickly cooked over high heat, is the usual way of cooking vegetables. The technique ensures that all-important flavor, color, and texture, as well as valuable nutrients, are preserved.

Salads as we know them in the West do not feature greatly on the Chinese menu, except perhaps in the Canton region, where chefs are more inclined to try out new ideas from abroad. However, many lightly cooked vegetable dishes can be classified as salads if they are cooled and lightly tossed in a dressing.

Tofu (bean curd) made from soybeans is eaten throughout China but is particularly popular in the north, where soybeans are an important crop. Hot-and-Sour Soup with Tofu, and Mushroom and Tofu Firepot are typical of hearty Mongolian cuisine. In regions where wheat is the staple, you'll find vegetable and noodle combinations instead of rice. Try Sweet-and-Sour Vegetables on Noodle Pancakes, or Chengdu Noodles in Sesame Sauce—a spicy Sichuan dish that is traditionally eaten cold.

Hot-and-Sour Soup with Tofu

SERVES 4

3 strips of lime zest
2 garlic cloves, peeled
2 slices fresh ginger
4 cups chicken stock
1 tbsp vegetable oil
6 oz/175 g firm tofu, drained and cubed
7 oz/200 g fine egg noodles
1½ cups sliced shiitake mushrooms

1 fresh red chile, seeded and sliced
4 scallions, sliced
1 tsp light soy sauce
juice of 1 lime
1 tsp Chinese rice wine
1 tsp sesame oil
chopped fresh cilantro, to garnish

1. Put the lime zest, garlic, and ginger into a large pan with the stock and bring to a boil. Reduce the heat and let simmer for 5 minutes. Remove the lime zest, garlic, and ginger with a slotted spoon and discard.

2. Meanwhile, heat the vegetable oil in a large skillet over high heat, add the tofu, and cook, turning frequently, until golden. Remove the tofu from the skillet and drain on paper towels.

3. Add the noodles, mushrooms, and chile to the stock and let simmer for 3 minutes.

4. Add the tofu, scallions, soy sauce, lime juice, rice wine, and sesame oil and briefly heat through.

5. Divide the soup among 4 warmed bowls, sprinkle over the cilantro, and serve immediately.

Mushroom and Ginger Soup

SERVES 4

½ oz/15 g dried Chinese mushrooms or
    4½ oz/125 g portobello or cremini
    mushrooms
4 cups hot vegetable stock
4½ oz/125 g thin egg noodles
2 tsp corn oil

3 garlic cloves, crushed
1-inch/2.5-cm piece fresh ginger,
    finely shredded
1 tsp light soy sauce
1¼ cups bean sprouts
fresh cilantro leaves, to garnish

1. Soak the dried Chinese mushrooms for at least 30 minutes in 1¼ cups of the hot stock. Drain the mushrooms and reserve the stock. Remove the stems of the mushrooms and discard. Slice the caps and reserve.

2. Cook the noodles according to the directions on the package. Drain well, rinse under cold water, and drain again. Set aside.

3. Heat the oil in a preheated wok or large, heavy-bottom skillet over high heat. Add the garlic and ginger, stir, and add the mushrooms. Stir over high heat for 2 minutes.

4. Add the remaining stock with the reserved mushroom soaking liquid and bring to a boil. Add the soy sauce. Stir in the bean sprouts and cook until tender.

5. Divide the noodles among 4 serving bowls and ladle the soup on top. Garnish with cilantro leaves and serve immediately.

Classic Stir-Fried Vegetables

SERVES 4

3 tbsp sesame oil

8 scallions, chopped

1 garlic clove, crushed

1 tbsp grated fresh ginger

1 head of broccoli, cut into florets

1 yellow or orange bell pepper, seeded and coarsely chopped

1 cup shredded red cabbage

4½ oz/125 g baby corn

2 cups thinly sliced portobello mushrooms

1⅓ cups fresh bean sprouts

9 oz/250 g canned water chestnuts, drained

4 tsp light soy sauce

1. Heat 2 tablespoons of the oil in a large skillet or wok over high heat. Stir-fry two thirds of the scallions with the garlic and ginger for 30 seconds.

2. Add the broccoli, bell pepper, and red cabbage and stir-fry for 1–2 minutes. Mix in the baby corn and mushrooms and stir-fry for an additional 1–2 minutes.

3. Finally, add the bean sprouts and water chestnuts and cook for an additional 2 minutes. Pour in the soy sauce and stir well.

4. Transfer to warmed dishes and serve immediately, garnished with the remaining scallions.

Bamboo Shoots with Tofu

SERVES 4–6

3 dried Chinese mushrooms, soaked in warm water for 20 minutes

1 cup baby bok choy (if unavailable use 1 head regular bok choy, thickly sliced)

1 lb/450 g firm tofu, drained and cut into 1-inch/2.5-cm squares

1 tbsp vegetable or peanut oil, plus extra for deep-frying

½ cup fresh or canned bamboo shoots, rinsed and finely sliced (if using fresh shoots, boil in water first for 30 minutes)

1 tsp oyster sauce

1 tsp light soy sauce

1. Squeeze out any excess water from the mushrooms and finely slice, discarding any tough stems.

2. Blanch the bok choy in a large pan of boiling water for 30 seconds. Drain and set aside.

3. Heat enough oil for deep-frying in a wok, deep-fat fryer, or large, heavy-bottom pan to 350–375°F/ 180–190°C, or until a cube of bread browns in 30 seconds. Fry the tofu until golden brown. Remove, drain on paper towels, and set aside.

4. In a preheated wok or deep pan, heat the 1 tablespoon of oil, toss in the mushrooms and bok choy, and stir. Add the tofu and bamboo shoots with the oyster sauce and soy sauce. Heat through and serve.

Spicy Tofu

SERVES 4

9 oz/250 g firm tofu, rinsed, drained, and cut
    into ½-inch/1-cm cubes

4 tbsp peanut oil

1 tbsp grated fresh ginger

3 garlic cloves, crushed

4 scallions, thinly sliced

1 head of broccoli, cut into florets

1 carrot, cut into batons

1 yellow bell pepper, seeded and thinly sliced

2¾ cups thinly sliced shiitake mushrooms

cooked rice, to serve

MARINADE

5 tbsp vegetable stock

2 tsp cornstarch

2 tbsp light soy sauce

1 tbsp superfine sugar

pinch of chile flakes

1. To make the marinade, mix the stock, cornstarch, soy sauce, sugar, and chile flakes together
   in a large bowl. Add the tofu and toss well to cover in the marinade. Set aside to marinate for
   20 minutes.

2. In a large skillet or wok, heat 2 tablespoons of the oil and stir-fry the tofu with its marinade until
   brown and crispy. Remove from the skillet and set aside.

3. Heat the remaining oil in the skillet and stir-fry the ginger, garlic, and scallions for 30 seconds. Add
   the broccoli, carrot, bell pepper, and mushrooms and cook for 5–6 minutes. Return the tofu to the
   skillet and stir-fry to heat through. Serve immediately with rice.

Mixed Vegetables with Quick-Fried Basil

SERVES 4

2 tbsp vegetable or peanut oil, plus extra for
  shallow-frying
2 garlic cloves, chopped
1 onion, sliced
4 oz/115 g baby corn, cut in half diagonally
½ cucumber, peeled, halved,
  seeded, and sliced
8 oz/225 g canned water chestnuts,
  drained and rinsed

¾ cup snow peas
2 cups shiitake mushrooms, halved
1 red bell pepper, seeded and thinly sliced
1 tbsp light brown sugar
2 tbsp light soy sauce
1 tbsp fish sauce
1 tbsp rice vinegar
8–12 sprigs fresh Thai basil
cooked rice, to serve

1. Heat the oil in a wok and stir-fry the garlic and onion for 1–2 minutes. Add the baby corn, cucumber, water chestnuts, snow peas, mushrooms, and bell pepper and stir-fry for 2–3 minutes, until starting to soften.

2. Add the sugar, soy sauce, fish sauce, and vinegar and gradually bring to a boil. Let simmer for 1–2 minutes.

3. Meanwhile, heat enough oil for shallow-frying in a wok. When hot, add the basil sprigs and cook for 20–30 seconds, until crisp. Remove with a slotted spoon and drain on paper towels.

4. Garnish the vegetable stir-fry with the crispy basil and serve immediately with rice.

Oyster Mushrooms and Vegetables with Peanut Chili Sauce

SERVES 4

1 tbsp vegetable or peanut oil
4 scallions, finely sliced
1 carrot, cut into thin strips
1 zucchini, cut into thin strips
½ head of broccoli, cut into florets
9 cups oyster mushrooms, thinly sliced

2 tbsp crunchy peanut butter
1 tsp chili powder, or to taste
3 tbsp water
cooked rice, to serve
lime wedges, to garnish

1. Heat the oil in a wok until almost smoking. Stir-fry the scallions for 1 minute. Add the carrot and zucchini and stir-fry for 1 minute, then add the broccoli and cook for an additional minute.

2. Stir in the mushrooms and cook until they have softened and at least half the liquid they produce has evaporated. Add the peanut butter and stir well. Season with the chili powder to taste. Finally, add the water and cook for an additional minute.

3. Serve with rice and garnish with lime wedges.

Broccoli and Snow Pea Stir-Fry

SERVES 4

2 tbsp vegetable or peanut oil

dash of sesame oil

1 garlic clove, finely chopped

1½ cups small broccoli florets

1 cup snow peas

3 cups thickly sliced Chinese cabbage

5–6 scallions, finely chopped

½ tsp salt

2 tbsp light soy sauce

1 tbsp Chinese rice wine

1 tsp sesame seeds, lightly toasted

1. In a preheated wok, heat the oils, then add the garlic and stir-fry vigorously. Add all the vegetables and salt and stir-fry over high heat, tossing rapidly, for about 3 minutes.

2. Pour in the soy sauce and rice wine and cook for an additional 2 minutes. Sprinkle with the sesame seeds and serve hot.

Choy Sum in Oyster Sauce

SERVES 4–6

10½ oz/300 g choy sum
1 tbsp vegetable or peanut oil

1 tsp finely chopped garlic
1 tbsp oyster sauce

1. Blanch the choy sum in a large pan of boiling water for 30 seconds. Drain and set aside.

2. In a preheated wok or deep pan, heat the oil and stir-fry the garlic until fragrant. Add the choy sum and toss for 1 minute. Stir in the oyster sauce and serve.

Eggplants With Red Bell Pepper

SERVES 4

3 tbsp vegetable or peanut oil

1 garlic clove, finely chopped

3 eggplants, halved lengthwise and cut diagonally into 1-inch/2.5-cm pieces

1 tsp white rice vinegar

1 red bell pepper, seeded and finely sliced

2 tbsp light soy sauce

1 tsp sugar

1 tbsp finely chopped cilantro leaves (optional), to garnish

1. In a preheated wok or deep pan, heat the oil. When it begins to smoke, toss in the garlic and stir-fry until fragrant, then add the eggplants. Stir-fry for 30 seconds, then add the vinegar. Turn down the heat and cook, covered, for 5 minutes, stirring from time to time.

2. When the eggplant pieces are soft, add the bell pepper and stir. Add the soy sauce and sugar and cook, uncovered, for 2 minutes.

3. Turn off the heat and let rest for 2 minutes. Transfer to a dish, then garnish with cilantro and serve.

Stuffed Eggplant with Spicy Sauce

SERVES 5–6

BATTER

⅔ cup chickpea flour

⅓ cup all-purpose flour

pinch of salt

1 egg, beaten

1¼ cups very cold water

STUFFING

3½ oz/100 g ground pork

½ tsp finely chopped scallion

½ tsp finely chopped fresh ginger

dash of Chinese rice wine

pinch of white pepper

pinch of salt

SPICY SAUCE

2-inch/5-cm piece fresh ginger

2 large garlic cloves

2 tbsp vegetable or peanut oil

3 tbsp chili bean sauce

1 tsp white rice vinegar

2 tsp sugar

⅔ cup chicken stock

2 large eggplants, cut into
   1½ inch/4 cm thick slices

vegetable or peanut oil, for deep-frying

1. To prepare the batter, sift together the flours and salt into a large bowl. Stir in the egg, then gradually add the water. Beat for at least 5 minutes, or until the batter is smooth and thick. Let rest in the refrigerator.

2. To prepare the stuffing, mix together all the ingredients and let stand for 20 minutes.

3. Make a small incision—cut less than halfway through—on the side of each eggplant slice. Stuff about ½ teaspoon of the pork stuffing into the incision, smoothing the surface with a knife to remove any excess.

4. Heat enough oil for deep-frying in a wok, deep-fat fryer, or large, heavy-bottom pan to 350–375°F/ 180–190°C, or until a cube of bread browns in 30 seconds. Dip each eggplant slice into the batter and lower straight into the oil. Cook for about 10 minutes, or until golden brown. Drain on paper towels and arrange in a bowl or on a serving plate.

5. Grate the ginger and garlic for the sauce on a very fine grater, discarding the fibrous parts left on top of the grater and reserving the juices.

6. Heat the oil in a preheated wok or deep pan. Add the chili bean sauce and stir for 1 minute, then reduce the heat. Add the ginger and garlic juice and stir-fry for 1 minute, then add the vinegar and sugar and cook for 2 minutes. Finally, add the stock and simmer for 2 minutes. Serve the stuffed eggplant slices with the sauce.

Sweet-and-Sour Vegetables on Noodle Pancakes

SERVES 4

4 oz/115 g thin rice noodles

2 lb/900 g selection of vegetables, such as carrots, baby corn, mushrooms, broccoli, snow peas, and onions

6 eggs

4 scallions, sliced diagonally

2½ tbsp peanut or corn oil

3½ oz/100 g canned bamboo shoots, drained

scant 1 cup store-bought sweet-and-sour sauce

salt and pepper

1. Soak the noodles in enough lukewarm water to cover and let stand for 20 minutes, until softened. Alternatively, cook according to the directions on the package. Drain well and use scissors to cut into 3-inch/7.5-cm pieces, then set aside.

2. Meanwhile, prepare the vegetables as necessary and chop into equal-size chunks.

3. Beat the eggs in a large bowl, then stir in the noodles and scallions and season to taste with salt and pepper. Heat an 8-inch/20-cm skillet over high heat. Add 1 tablespoon of the oil and swirl it around. Pour in one quarter of the egg mixture and tilt the skillet so it covers the bottom. Reduce the heat to medium and cook for 1 minute, or until the thin pancake is set. Flip it over and continue cooking until the pancake is set. Keep warm in a low oven while you make 3 more pancakes.

4. Heat a wok or large skillet over high heat. Add the remaining oil and heat until it shimmers. Add the thickest vegetables, such as carrots, first and stir-fry for 30 seconds. Gradually add the remaining vegetables and the bamboo shoots. Stir in the sauce and stir-fry until all the vegetables are tender and the sauce is hot. Spoon the vegetables and sauce over the pancakes and serve.

Sweet-and-Sour Vegetables with Cashew Nuts

SERVES 4

1 tbsp vegetable or peanut oil
1 tsp chili oil
2 onions, sliced
2 carrots, thinly sliced
2 zucchini, thinly sliced
1 small head of broccoli, cut into small florets

2¼ cups sliced mushrooms
2 heads of baby bok choy, sliced
2 tbsp light brown sugar
2 tbsp light soy sauce
1 tbsp rice vinegar
scant ½ cup cashew nuts

1. Heat the oils in a wok and stir-fry the onions for 1–2 minutes, until they start to soften.

2. Add the carrots, zucchini, and broccoli and stir-fry for 2–3 minutes. Add the mushrooms, bok choy, sugar, soy sauce, and vinegar and stir-fry for 1–2 minutes.

3. Meanwhile, dry-fry the cashew nuts in a small skillet until lightly colored. Sprinkle the cashew nuts over the stir-fry and serve immediately.

Mushroom and Tofu Firepot

SERVES 4

2 oz/55 g dried Chinese mushrooms

4 oz/115 g firm tofu, drained

2 tbsp sweet chili sauce

2 tbsp peanut or corn oil

2 large garlic cloves, chopped

½-inch/1-cm piece fresh ginger, finely chopped

1 red onion, sliced

½ tbsp Sichuan peppers, lightly crushed

4 oz/115 g canned straw mushrooms, drained and rinsed

1 star anise

pinch of sugar

soy sauce, to taste

4 oz/115 g thin rice noodles

1. Soak the mushrooms in enough boiling water to cover for 20 minutes, or until softened. Cut the tofu into bite-size chunks and stir with the sweet chili sauce until coated, then let marinate.

2. Strain the soaked mushrooms through a strainer lined with a paper towel, reserving the soaking liquid. Heat the oil in a medium flameproof casserole or large skillet with a lid. Add the garlic and ginger and stir them around for 30 seconds. Add the onion and peppers and keep stirring until the onion is almost tender. Add the tofu, the soaked mushrooms, and the straw mushrooms and stir around carefully so the tofu doesn't break up.

3. Add the reserved strained mushroom soaking liquid to the wok with just enough water to cover the tofu mixture. Stir in the star anise and sugar with several dashes of soy sauce, or to taste. Bring to a boil, then reduce the heat to the lowest setting, cover, and let simmer for 5 minutes. Add the noodles to the wok, re-cover, and simmer for an additional 5 minutes, or until the noodles are tender. The noodles should be covered with liquid, so add extra water at this point, if necessary. Use a fork or wooden spoon to stir the noodles into the other ingredients. Serve immediately.

Braised Straw Mushrooms

SERVES 4

1 tbsp vegetable or peanut oil

1 tsp finely chopped garlic

6 oz/175 g straw mushrooms,
washed but left whole

2 tsp fermented black beans,
rinsed and lightly mashed

1 tsp sugar

1 tbsp light soy sauce

1 tsp dark soy sauce

1. Heat the oil in a small flameproof casserole. Cook the garlic until fragrant, then add the mushrooms and stir well to coat in the oil.

2. Add the beans, sugar, and soy sauces, then reduce the heat and simmer, covered, for about 10 minutes, or until the mushrooms have softened. Serve immediately.

Vegetable and Coconut Curry

SERVES 4

1 onion, coarsely chopped

3 garlic cloves, thinly sliced

1-inch/2.5-cm piece fresh ginger, thinly sliced

2 fresh green chiles, seeded and finely chopped

1 tbsp vegetable oil

1 tsp ground turmeric

1 tsp ground coriander

1 tsp ground cumin

2 lb 4 oz/1 kg mixed vegetables, such as cauliflower, zucchini, potatoes, carrots, and green beans, cut into chunks

scant 1 cup coconut cream or coconut milk

salt and pepper

2 tbsp chopped fresh cilantro, to garnish

cooked rice, to serve

1. Put the onion, garlic, ginger, and chiles in a food processor and process until almost smooth.

2. Heat the oil in a large, heavy-bottom pan over low–medium heat, add the onion mixture, and cook, stirring constantly, for 5 minutes.

3. Add the turmeric, coriander, and cumin and cook, stirring frequently, for 3–4 minutes. Add the vegetables and stir to coat in the spice paste.

4. Add the coconut cream to the vegetables, cover, and let simmer for 30–40 minutes, until the vegetables are tender.

5. Season to taste with salt and pepper, garnish with the cilantro, and serve with rice.

Egg Fu Yung

SERVES 4–6

2 eggs

½ tsp salt

pinch of white pepper

1 tsp butter

2 tbsp vegetable or peanut oil

1 tsp finely chopped garlic

1 small onion, finely sliced

1 green bell pepper, finely sliced

2¼ cups cooked rice, chilled

1 tbsp light soy sauce

1 tbsp finely chopped scallion

1 cup bean sprouts

2 drops of sesame oil

1. Beat the eggs with the salt and pepper. Heat the butter in a skillet and pour in the eggs. Cook as an omelet, until set, then remove from the pan and cut into slivers.

2. In a preheated wok or deep pan, heat the oil and stir-fry the garlic until fragrant. Add the onion and stir-fry for 1 minute, then add the bell pepper and stir for an additional minute. Stir in the rice and, when the grains are separated, stir in the soy sauce and cook for 1 minute.

3. Add the scallion and egg strips and stir well, then add the bean sprouts and sesame oil. Stir-fry for 1 minute and serve.

Chengdu Noodles in Sesame Sauce

SERVES 4–6

14 oz/400 g thin wheat flour noodles
1 cup bean sprouts
1 tbsp finely chopped scallion
2 tbsp sesame seeds

SAUCE
1 tbsp sugar
1 tbsp sesame oil
2 oz/55 g sesame paste
1 tbsp chili oil
2 tsp dark soy sauce
1 tbsp black Chinese vinegar

1. Cook the noodles according to the directions on the package. When cooked, rinse under cold water and set aside. Blanch the bean sprouts in a large pan of boiling water for 30 seconds. Drain and set aside.

2. To prepare the sauce, beat all the ingredients together until the sauce is smooth and thick.

3. To serve, toss the noodles in the sauce, stir in the bean sprouts, and sprinkle with the scallion and sesame seeds.

Side Dishes and Desserts

A Chinese meal usually includes an appetizing selection of small dishes, similar to hors d'oeuvres in the West. Typical are tasty meat or vegetables packaged in crisp-fried pastry wrappers—egg rolls or deep-fried wontons, for example—often served with a simple dipping sauce. Shrimp Toasts and spicy Soy Chicken Wings are also popular. A few simple vegetable side dishes, such as Stir-Fried Bean Sprouts or Spicy Green Beans, are also part of a typical meal.

Rice, of course, is an essential and satisfying part of most Chinese meals. Plainly steamed, it provides a complementary texture to other ingredients and absorbs the stronger flavors of well-seasoned meat and fish. Also popular, both at home and in restaurants, is Egg-Fried

Rice. This dish is a good way of using up leftover rice and can be easily transformed into a filling main dish with the addition of a little meat or seafood and some vegetables.

Desserts do not feature largely in China, although at banquets or formal dinners sweet dishes are served to punctuate the long succession of savory dishes. Fresh fruit, either on its own or as part of an impressive fruit salad, might also be served on such occasions. Irresistible Toffee Bananas and Toffee Apple Slices are popular, particularly in Peking, where chefs are adept at caramelizing sugar in hot oil. Sweet dishes are more likely to be eaten separately from a meal as between-meal snacks.

Pork and Shrimp Egg Rolls

MAKES 20–25

6 dried Chinese mushrooms, soaked in warm water for 20 minutes

1 tbsp vegetable or peanut oil, plus extra for deep-frying

8 oz/225 g ground pork

1 tsp dark soy sauce

1 cup fresh or canned bamboo shoots, rinsed and julienned (if using fresh shoots, boil in water first for 30 minutes)

pinch of salt

3½ oz/100 g shrimp, peeled, deveined, and chopped

generous 1½ cups bean sprouts, coarsely chopped

1 tbsp finely chopped scallion

25 egg roll wrappers

1 egg white, lightly beaten

1. Squeeze out any excess water from the mushrooms and finely slice, discarding any tough stems.

2. In a preheated wok or deep pan, heat the tablespoon of oil and stir-fry the pork until it changes color. Add the soy sauce, bamboo shoots, mushrooms, and salt. Stir over high heat for 3 minutes.

3. Add the shrimp and cook for 2 minutes, then add the bean sprouts and cook for an additional minute. Remove from the heat and stir in the scallion. Let cool.

4. Place a tablespoon of the mixture toward the bottom of a wrapper. Roll once to secure the filling, then fold in the sides to create a 4 inch/10 cm long egg roll and continue to roll up. Seal with egg white.

5. Heat enough oil for deep-frying in a wok, deep-fat fryer, or large, heavy-bottom pan to 350–375°F/ 180–190°C, or until a cube of bread browns in 30 seconds. Cook the egg rolls, in batches, for about 5 minutes, until golden brown and crispy.

Vegetarian Egg Rolls

MAKES 20

6 dried Chinese mushrooms, soaked in warm
water for 20 minutes

2 oz/55 g thin rice noodles, soaked in warm
water for 20 minutes

2 tbsp vegetable or peanut oil, plus extra
for greasing

1 tbsp finely chopped fresh ginger

generous ⅔ cup julienned carrot

scant 1 cup finely shredded cabbage

1 tbsp finely sliced scallion

1 tbsp light soy sauce

3 oz/85 g tofu, drained and cut into
small cubes

½ tsp salt

pinch of white pepper

pinch of sugar

20 egg roll wrappers

1 egg white, lightly beaten

dark soy sauce, to serve

1. Squeeze out any excess water from the mushrooms and finely chop, discarding any tough stems.
   Drain the noodles and coarsely chop.

2. In a preheated wok or deep pan, heat the 2 tablespoons of oil, then toss in the ginger and cook
   until fragrant. Add the mushrooms and stir for about 2 minutes. Add the carrot, cabbage, and
   scallion and stir-fry for 1 minute. Add the noodles and light soy sauce and stir-fry for 1 minute. Add
   the tofu and cook for an additional minute. Season with the salt, pepper, and sugar and mix well.
   Continue cooking for 1–2 minutes, or until the carrot has softened. Remove from the heat and let
   the mixture cool.

3. Place a scant tablespoon of the mixture toward the bottom of a wrapper. Roll once to secure the
   filling, then fold in the sides to create a 4 inch/10 cm long egg roll and continue to roll up. Seal with
   egg white.

4. Heat enough oil for deep-frying in a wok, deep-fat fryer, or large, heavy-bottom pan to 350–375°F/
   180–190°C, or until a cube of bread browns in 30 seconds. Without overcrowding the pan, cook the
   rolls for about 5 minutes, or until golden brown and crispy. Serve with dark soy sauce for dipping.

Soy Chicken Wings

SERVES 3–4

9 oz/250 g chicken wings

1 cup water

1 tbsp sliced scallion

1-inch/2.5-cm piece fresh ginger,
   cut into 4 slices

2 tbsp light soy sauce

½ tsp dark soy sauce

1 star anise

1 tsp sugar

1. Wash and dry the chicken wings. Bring the water to a boil in a small pan, then add the chicken, scallion, and ginger and bring back to a boil.

2. Add the remaining ingredients, then cover and simmer for 30 minutes. Meanwhile, preheat the oven to 350°F/180°C.

3. Remove the chicken wings with a slotted spoon and drain on paper towels. Spread out in a single layer in a roasting pan and cook in the preheated oven for 15–20 minutes, until lightly browned. Serve hot.

Shrimp Toasts

MAKES 16

3½ oz/100g shrimp, peeled and deveined
2 egg whites
2 tbsp cornstarch
½ tsp sugar

pinch of salt
2 tbsp finely chopped cilantro leaves
2 slices day-old white bread
vegetable or peanut oil, for deep-frying

1. Pound the shrimp to a paste with a pestle or process briefly in a food processor.

2. Mix the shrimp with 1 of the egg whites and 1 tablespoon of the cornstarch. Add the sugar and salt and stir in the cilantro. Mix the remaining egg white with the remaining cornstarch.

3. Remove the crusts from the bread and cut each slice into 8 triangles. Brush the top of each piece with the egg white-and-cornstarch mixture, then add 1 teaspoon of the shrimp mixture. Smooth the top.

4. Heat enough oil for deep-frying in a wok, deep-fat fryer, or large, heavy-bottom pan to 350–375°F/ 180–190°C, or until a cube of bread browns in 30 seconds. Without overcrowding the wok, cook the toasts, shrimp-side up, for about 2 minutes. Turn and cook for an additional 2 minutes, or until beginning to turn golden brown. Remove with a slotted spoon, drain on paper towels, and serve warm.

Stir-Fried Broccoli

SERVES 4

2 tbsp vegetable oil

2 medium heads of broccoli, cut into florets

2 tbsp light soy sauce

1 tsp cornstarch

1 tbsp superfine sugar

1 tsp grated fresh ginger

1 garlic clove, crushed

pinch of hot chile flakes

1 tsp toasted sesame seeds, to garnish

1. In a large skillet or wok, heat the oil until almost smoking. Stir-fry the broccoli for 4–5 minutes.

2. In a small bowl, combine the soy sauce, cornstarch, sugar, ginger, garlic, and chile flakes. Add the mixture to the broccoli. Cook over a gentle heat, stirring constantly, for 2–3 minutes, until the sauce thickens slightly.

3. Transfer to a serving dish, garnish with the sesame seeds, and serve immediately.

Stir-Fried Bean Sprouts

1 tbsp vegetable or peanut oil
generous 1½ cups bean sprouts
2 tbsp finely chopped scallion

½ tsp salt
pinch of sugar

1. In a preheated wok or deep pan, heat the oil and stir-fry the bean sprouts with the scallion for about 1 minute. Add the salt and sugar and stir. Serve immediately.

Spicy Green Beans

SERVES 4

generous 1¼ cups green beans, trimmed and
   cut diagonally into 3–4 pieces

2 tbsp vegetable or peanut oil

4 dried chiles, cut into 2–3 pieces

½ tsp Sichuan peppers

1 garlic clove, finely sliced

6 thin slices of fresh ginger

2 scallions, white part only, cut diagonally into
   thin pieces

pinch of sea salt

1. Blanch the beans in a large pan of boiling water for 30 seconds. Drain and set aside.

2. In a preheated wok, heat 1 tablespoon of the oil. Over low heat, stir-fry the beans for about
   5 minutes, or until they are beginning to wrinkle. Remove from the wok and set aside.

3. Add the remaining oil to the wok and stir-fry the chiles and peppers until they are fragrant. Add the
   garlic, ginger, and scallions and stir-fry until they begin to soften. Add the beans and toss to mix,
   then add the sea salt and serve immediately on warmed plates.

Stir-Fried Green Beans with Red Bell Pepper

SERVES 4–6

10 oz/280 g green beans, cut into
    2½-inch/6-cm lengths
1 tbsp vegetable or peanut oil

1 red bell pepper, seeded and thinly sliced
pinch of salt
pinch of sugar

1. Blanch the beans in a large pan of boiling water for 30 seconds. Drain and set aside.

2. In a preheated wok, heat the oil and stir-fry the beans for 1 minute over high heat. Add the bell pepper and stir-fry for an additional minute. Sprinkle the salt and sugar on top and serve.

Hot-and-Sour Cabbage

SERVES 4

1 small head of firm white cabbage
1 tbsp vegetable or peanut oil
10 Sichuan peppers or more, to taste
3 dried chiles, coarsely chopped

½ tsp salt
1 tsp white rice vinegar
dash of sesame oil
pinch of sugar

1. To prepare the cabbage, discard the outer leaves and tough stems. Chop the cabbage into 1¼-inch/ 3-cm squares, breaking up the chunks. Rinse thoroughly in cold water.

2. In a preheated wok, heat the vegetable oil and cook the peppers until fragrant. Stir in the chiles. Add the cabbage, a little at a time, together with the salt, and stir-fry for 2 minutes.

3. Add the vinegar, sesame oil, and sugar and cook for an additional minute, or until the cabbage is tender. Serve immediately on warmed plates.

Steamed White Rice

SERVES 3–4

generous 1 cup long-grain white rice

1. Place the rice in a strainer and wash under cold running water. Drain well.

2. Place the rice in a pan with the same volume of water plus a little extra (the water should just cover the rice). Bring to a boil, then cover and simmer for about 15 minutes.

3. Turn off the heat and let the rice continue to cook in its own steam for about 5 minutes. At this point, the grains should be cooked through but not sticking together. Serve.

Egg-Fried Rice

SERVES 4

2 tbsp vegetable or peanut oil
2 cups cooked rice, chilled

1 egg, well beaten

1. Heat the oil in a preheated wok or deep pan and stir-fry the rice for 1 minute, breaking it down as much as possible into individual grains.

2. Quickly add the egg, stirring to coat each piece of rice. Stir until the egg is cooked and the rice, as far as possible, is in single grains. Serve the rice immediately.

Tea-Scented Eggs

SERVES 6

6 eggs   2 tbsp black tea leaves

1. Bring a pan of water to a boil and cook the eggs for 10 minutes. Remove the eggs from the pan and lightly crack the shells with the back of a spoon.

2. Bring the water back to a boil and simmer the tea leaves for 5 minutes. Turn off the heat. Place the eggs in the tea and let stand until the tea has cooled.

3. Serve the eggs whole for breakfast or as part of a meal.

Pears in Honey Syrup

SERVES 4

4 medium-ripe pears
generous ¾ cup water

1 tsp sugar
1 tbsp honey

1. Peel each pear, leaving the stem intact. Wrap each in aluminum foil and place in a pan with the stems resting on the side of the pan. Add enough water to cover at least half of the height of the pears. Bring to a boil and simmer for 30 minutes. Remove the pears from the pan and carefully remove the aluminum foil, reserving any juices. Set the pears aside to cool.

2. Bring the measured water to a boil. Add any pear juices, the sugar, and honey and boil for 5 minutes. Remove from the heat and let cool a little.

3. To serve, place each pear in a small individual dish. Pour a little syrup over each and serve just warm.

Fresh Fruit Salad with Lemon Juice

SERVES 4–6

2 tbsp sugar

1 lb/450 g mixed melons, peeled, seeded, and cut into balls or cubes

2 bananas, sliced

juice of 1 lemon

1. In a large bowl, sprinkle the sugar over the melon pieces. Toss the banana in the lemon juice and add to the melon, then serve immediately.

Mango Pudding

SERVES 6

1 oz/25 g sago, soaked in water for at least 20 minutes

1 cup warm water

2 tbsp sugar

1 large, ripe mango, about 10 oz/280 g

generous ¾ cup heavy cream

1 tbsp powdered gelatin, dissolved in 1 cup warm water

1. Drain the sago and place in a pan with the warm water. Bring to a boil and then cook over low heat for 10 minutes, stirring frequently until thick. Stir in the sugar and let cool.

2. Peel the mango and slice off the flesh from the pit. Reserving a few small slices for decoration, blend the mango to a smooth paste in a food processor or blender. Stir in the cream and add the gelatin.

3. Add the sago to the mango mixture and mix well. Pour into 6 small bowls and refrigerate until set. Decorate with the reserved mango slices before serving.

Toffee Bananas

SERVES 4

½ cup self-rising flour
1 egg, beaten
5 tbsp ice water
4 large, ripe bananas
3 tbsp lemon juice
2 tbsp rice flour
vegetable oil, for deep-frying

CARAMEL
generous ½ cup superfine sugar
4 tbsp ice water, plus an extra bowl
  of ice water for setting
2 tbsp sesame seeds

1. Sift the self-rising flour into a bowl. Make a well in the center, add the egg and the 5 tablespoons of iced water, and beat from the center outward, until combined into a smooth batter.

2. Peel the bananas and cut into 2-inch/5-cm pieces. Gently shape them into balls with your hands. Brush with lemon juice to prevent discoloration, then roll them in rice flour until coated.

3. Heat enough oil for deep-frying in a wok, deep-fat fryer, or large, heavy-bottom pan to 350–375°F/180–190°C, or until a cube of bread browns in 30 seconds. Coat the balls in the batter and cook, in batches, for about 2 minutes, until golden. Remove with a slotted spoon and drain on paper towels.

4. To make the caramel, put the sugar into a small pan over low heat. Add the 4 tablespoons of ice water and heat, stirring, until the sugar dissolves. Simmer for 5 minutes, remove from the heat, and stir in the sesame seeds. Toss the banana balls in the caramel, scoop them out, and drop into the bowl of ice water to set. Remove with a slotted spoon and divide among individual serving bowls. Serve immediately.

Banana and Coconut Fritters

SERVES 4

½ cup all-purpose flour
2 tbsp rice flour
1 tbsp superfine sugar
1 egg, separated
⅔ cup coconut milk
vegetable oil, for deep-frying
4 large bananas

TO DECORATE/SERVE
1 tsp confectioners' sugar
1 tsp ground cinnamon
lime wedges

1. Sift the all-purpose flour, rice flour, and superfine sugar into a bowl and make a well in the center. Add the egg yolk and coconut milk. Beat the mixture until a smooth, thick batter forms.

2. Beat the egg white in a clean, dry bowl until stiff enough to hold soft peaks. Fold it into the batter lightly and evenly.

3. Heat enough oil for deep-frying in a wok, deep-fat fryer, or large, heavy-bottom pan to 350–375°F/ 180–190°C, or until a cube of bread browns in 30 seconds. Cut the bananas in half, first lengthwise and then crosswise, then dip them quickly into the batter to coat them.

4. Drop the bananas carefully into the hot oil and deep-fry, in batches, for 2–3 minutes, until golden brown, turning once.

5. Remove with a slotted spoon and drain on paper towels. Sprinkle with confectioners' sugar and cinnamon and serve immediately with lime wedges for squeezing over.

Toffee Apple Slices

SERVES 6

4 apples, peeled, cored, and each cut into
   8 wedges
vegetable or peanut oil, for deep-frying

BATTER
⅔ cup all-purpose flour
1 egg, beaten
½ cup cold water

TOFFEE SYRUP
4 tbsp sesame oil
scant 1¼ cups sugar
2 tbsp sesame seeds, toasted

1. To prepare the batter, sift the flour into a bowl and stir in the egg. Slowly add the water, beating to give a smooth, thick batter. Dip each apple wedge into the batter.

2. Heat enough oil for deep-frying in a wok, deep-fat fryer, or large, heavy-bottom pan to 350–375°F/ 180–190°C, or until a cube of bread browns in 30 seconds. Deep-fry the apple wedges until golden brown. Drain on paper towels and set aside.

3. To make the toffee syrup, heat the sesame oil in a small, heavy-bottom pan and when beginning to smoke add the sugar, stirring constantly, until the mixture caramelizes and turns golden. Remove from the heat, then stir in the sesame seeds and pour into a large skillet.

4. Over low heat, place the apple wedges in the syrup, turning once. When coated, drop each wedge into a bowl of ice water to set. Remove with a slotted spoon and serve immediately.

Almond Dessert in Ginger Sauce

SERVES 6–8

3¾ cups water
⅛ oz/5 g agar
scant 1¼ cups sugar
½ cup evaporated milk
1 tsp almond extract

GINGER SAUCE
2½-inch/6-cm piece fresh ginger,
    coarsely chopped
3¾ cups water
generous ¼ cup light brown sugar

1. Bring the water to a boil in a pan. Add the agar and stir until dissolved. Stir in the sugar.

2. Pour through a strainer into a shallow dish. Pour in the evaporated milk, stirring constantly. When slightly cooled, stir in the almond extract. Let chill in the refrigerator until set.

3. To make the ginger sauce, boil the ginger, water, and brown sugar in a pan, covered, for at least 1½ hours, or until the sauce is golden in color. Discard the ginger.

4. Using a sharp knife, cut the almond dessert into thin slices and arrange in individual bowls. Pour over a little ginger sauce, warm or cold, and serve.

Index

reen

NEW DIRECTIONS IN SUSTAINABLE ARCHITECTURE

use

PUBLISHED BY:
Princeton Architectural Press
37 East Seventh Street
New York, New York 10003

Visit our web site at www.papress.com

© 2005 Princeton Architectural Press
First paperback edition, 2010
Printed and bound in China
13   4

This book was made possible by a
generous grant from the Graham
Foundation.

ACQUISITIONS EDITOR: Mark Lamster
PROJECT EDITOR: Nancy Eklund Later
DESIGN & TYPOGRAPHY: Pure+Applied, NYC

SPECIAL THANKS TO:
Nettie Aljian, Nicola Bednarek,
Janet Behning, Megan Carey, Penny
(Yuen Pik) Chu, Russell Fernandez,
Jan Haux, Clare Jacobson, John King,
Linda Lee, Katharine Myers, Lauren Nelson,
Jane Sheinman, Scott Tennent, Jennifer
Thompson, Joseph Weston, and
Deb Wood of Princeton Architectural Press
—Kevin C. Lippert, publisher

ISBN 978-1-56898-950-1

The Library of Congress has
catalogued the hardcover edition
as follows:
Stang, Alanna, 1970–
The green house: new directions in
sustainable architecture / Alanna Stang
and Christopher Hawthorne. —1st ed.
    192 p. : ill. (some col.) ; 24 cm.
ISBN 1-56898-481-2 (alk. paper)
1. Sustainable architecture—
Exhibitions. 2. Ecological houses—
Exhibitions.
I. Hawthorne, Christopher. II. Title.
NA2542.36.S73 2005
728′.37′09049—dc22
        2005000193

The Green House

Princeton Architectural Press
New York

The National Building Museum
Washington, D.C.

the g

ho

Alanna Stang and Christopher Hawthorne

For András,
Rachel, and Willa;
and for architects,
writers, and
environmentalists
to come

CONTENTS

ACKNOWLEDGMENTS

We are deeply grateful to the Graham Foundation for Advanced Studies in the Fine Arts for its early financial support of this project. We thank Mark Lamster for signing on when the ideas were just half-baked and Nancy Eklund Later for smart, clear-eyed edits, as well as their colleagues at Princeton Architectural Press. We're most appreciative of Paul Carlos and Urshula Barbour of Pure+Applied for giving the project such a fitting form. Their generous talent, keen insight, and tireless patience made the process as rewarding as the end product. We're also indebted to our editorial assistants on either coast, Michelle Maisto and Jessica Fine Kleinman, for their fine research and good humor; to Eve M. Kahn and Paul Goldberger for their hearty endorsements; to Jeanne Wikler, Robert Kloos, Johanna Lemola, and Jari Sinkari for helping bridge the gap to architects abroad; as well as to Ann Alter and Harrison Fraker. Finally, we thank each of the architects and photographers whose inspiring work is featured here, along with their staffs.

Alanna Stang and Christopher Hawthorne

This book, and the exhibition of the same name organized by the National Building Museum, advance a noble if slightly ironic cause—that of making "green" architecture utterly unremarkable. They do so by presenting exemplary projects that are remarkable as architecture, in which environmental responsibility is an integral, if not always obvious, aspect of their design.

A generation ago, the popular imagery of sustainable housing included steeply slanted roofs blanketed by solar panels, rustic walls peeking out above giant earthen berms, and the occasional architectural folly constructed of a motley collection of found items recycled into vernacular building materials. Many such overtly "Earth-friendly" structures were easily mocked by architectural purists, who decried what they saw as the triumph of mundane problem-solving over high-minded aesthetics. Nonetheless, these prototypical green houses played an important role in raising public awareness that the built environment was a significant contributor to the profound degradation and diminishment of limited natural resources.

As with many sociopolitical movements, this early period of radicalism, in which explicit display played a decisive role, was followed by one in which bits and pieces of the philosophy were assimilated into the mainstream, albeit often in a token manner. Some architects appropriated the "look" of environmentalism, perhaps by tossing a sunscreen on a building, but did so with little regard for its solar orientation. Others actively reacted against the movement, especially as historicism once again gained favor among architects and the general public and as developers, at least in the United States, provided eager customers with increasingly gigantic, detached houses.

The contents of this book and exhibition suggest that the sustainability movement, to use a now prevalent term, is reaching maturity. Many architects, engineers, planners, developers, and clients have come to think more strategically about the environmental implications of building, especially in the domestic realm. Moving well beyond the simplistic inclusion of a few green materials or features, they are increasingly conceiving of houses as coherent, holistic systems, with extended life cycles that must be considered throughout the design process. Environmental concerns inform the architecture, of course, but the results can be as aesthetically rich as even the most abstract or theoretical of projects. Sustainability thus assumes another dimension beyond its mere pragmatic and ethical dimensions.

At the National Building Museum, *The Green House: New Directions in Sustainable Architecture* is part of a series of exhibitions about sustainable design. The first of these, *Big & Green: Toward Sustainable Architecture in the 21st Century*, which was presented in 2003, examined skyscrapers and other large-scale structures that successfully address environmental concerns. The museum plans to continue to organize exhibitions and public programs exploring this vital topic and thereby to advocate a future in which environmental sensitivity may be safely assumed in all works of architecture.

Chase W. Rynd
Executive Director
National Building Museum

CAMERA-READY GREEN DESIGN

ONE AFTERNOON SEVERAL MONTHS AGO, we found ourselves waiting in the quiet, impossibly picturesque Swiss town of Domat/Ems to meet an architect named Dietrich Schwarz. Though still in his thirties, Schwarz has already earned a reputation as one of Switzerland's leading practitioners of the environmentally friendly approach to architecture known as sustainable, or "green," design. Using a combination of new, high-tech materials—some of his own invention—and old-fashioned architectural wisdom, he creates houses and other buildings that are snugly energy-efficient and sit lightly on the land.

We had arrived a bit early for our appointment at Schwarz's office, which takes up one half of a pair of shimmery steel-and-glass pavilions he designed in the mid-1990s, not long after finishing architecture school. Although it was a Sunday, and beautiful out, a few of Schwarz's twenty-something staffers were hard at work in the cool, dark interior, their faces lit by glowing computer monitors. One of them led us outside to a sunny courtyard between the buildings, where a modest fountain splashed, and within a couple of minutes Schwarz himself appeared. Though he had driven a short distance from his nearby home, he looked as though he'd come straight from Milan. His dark hair was artfully messy. Precisely edged sideburns curled across each cheek. He was wearing an impeccably tailored dress shirt, perfectly faded jeans, and black leather shoes with the almost violently pointed toes that were just then becoming fashionable.

Standing in front of his elegant, neo-modernist office, Schwarz was a picture of the up-to-date, ready to pose for a spread in *Wallpaper* or *Elle Decor*. At the same time, it became clear once he began talking that he wasn't embarrassed by the idea of passionate environmentalism, unlike many architects who think of themselves as operating close to the cutting edge (and fashion themselves accordingly). On the contrary: his childhood in

this idyllic part of the world has made him committed to an architecture that does its best to protect both the local and the global landscape. And by his own admission he is a zealot when it comes to finding and testing the latest sustainable building materials.

It was on that afternoon—probably at the moment Schwarz launched into an energetic description of Power Glass, a type of super-efficient solar paneling for which he has received a patent—that we realized just how quickly the walls between green architecture and high design were crumbling, opening up new opportunities for crossover between the two realms. That new traffic is particularly notable among residential architects. While green design is also growing quickly in the public and commercial spheres, houses offer an ideal testing ground for the latest in sustainable architecture. Relatively small and self-contained, and often funded by progressive private clients (as opposed to bottom-line–oriented commercial ones), they allow for a unique kind of architectural experimentation. Indeed, many architectural movements and breakthroughs have found their earliest expression in residential work; green architecture is only the latest.

What we soon discovered is that all over the world—but particularly in northern Europe,

Canada, the United States, Japan, and Australia—residential architects are combining eye-catching contemporary architecture with sustainability. For a book that we believe is the first of its kind, we set out to select the finest examples of this new confluence and explain how each of them came into being: who commissioned these houses and apartment blocks, how their designs evolved, and how their architects and builders managed to balance environmental and aesthetic concerns so effectively.

The more we began to search for such projects, the more we realized not just how many are out there (indeed, we ended up with more qualified projects than we had pages to show them on) but the remarkable regional and architectural variety they represent. Green houses now rise from tightly packed city streets as well as from lush hillsides and rocky seashores. They are single-family dwellings and subsidized apartments, primary residences and weekend getaways. They are sheathed in glass, in bamboo, in synthetic panels made from recycled newspaper. They take their aesthetic cues from primitive dwellings, from organic forms, and, significantly, from architectural predecessors who include the founders of the Bauhaus as surely as Paolo Soleri or Frank Lloyd Wright. In fact, it is becoming impossible to ignore how many green houses are now being designed in the sleek, ornament-free style that has once again become the prevailing architectural approach among high-end architects, particularly younger ones in America and Europe. For the first time in the history of the green design movement, sustainability is being embraced by the very same architects who set the field's stylistic and theoretical agendas.

In addition to Dietrich Schwarz's corner of Switzerland, our search for the houses that fill the following pages took us to locations all around the world. On the edge of Lake Washington, near Seattle, we discovered a new house by the well-known Pacific Northwest firm Olson Sundberg Kundig Allen. Its design is anchored by a curving u-shaped wall that is an engaging sculptural element and—because it both conducts cool air in the summer and bounces sunlight back into the interior in winter—the key to its remarkable energy-efficiency. Down the coast in Marin County, California, we met Michelle Kaufmann, who had recently left a job in Frank Gehry's office to start her own firm. Kaufmann has designed the modular Glide House, the first mass-produced green home. It can be custom-ordered and then trucked directly

to a building site to be constructed in a matter of weeks; it is already on the market for roughly $120 per square foot, a bargain given the high quality of its materials and design.

A little further south, we went to see Colorado Court, a forty-four-unit low-income apartment complex in Santa Monica designed by the well-regarded firm Pugh + Scarpa. On the opposite coast, we followed the progress of Rafael Pelli's green apartment tower in Manhattan. The Solaire is the first sustainable residential project of its size or ambition in an American city. And a couple hours north of New York City, we discovered that Steven Holl, a much-lauded architect whose name has rarely, if ever, been mentioned in connection with green design, had designed an addition to his own weekend home that includes a long list of sustainable elements, from solar panels to an inventive natural-ventilation system.

In Europe, we found sustainable dwellings with a level of architectural and environmental sophistication that puts most green buildings in the United States to shame. It is well known that many European countries have building codes that pay significantly more attention to issues of sustainability than those in the United States. Less remarked upon, at least in the American press, has been Europe's substantial investment in new housing that meets stringent sustainability benchmarks. Cities like Helsinki and Stockholm have dedicated huge and valuable swaths of land to green developments, some of which contain several thousand units of housing.

Not all the European projects that fill these pages are publicly subsidized, to be sure. On a steep hillside overlooking Stuttgart, we toured the jaw-dropping R128, a steel-and-glass box designed by the German engineer Werner Sobek as his family residence. Since the days of Mies van der Rohe's Farnsworth House in Plano, Illinois, and its see-through sibling in New Canaan, Connecticut, by Philip Johnson (both finished around 1950), the glass house has stood as the epitome of the modernist aesthetic; unfortunately, such dwellings have often been both uncomfortable to live in (too hot in summer, too cold in winter) and, with their high heating and cooling bills and insensitivity to site, hardly kind to the environment either. Sobek set himself the stiff challenge of starting with the famous typology of the glass house and then making it supremely energy-efficient. His design has certainly been a success in that regard: during

R128, by Werner Sobek.

much of the year, the solar panels on the roof provide more electricity than he and his family need to operate the house. (They sell the excess back to the local power company.) Sobek is not the first architect to design a house that creates more power than it uses. But to combine that efficiency with exquisitely proportioned, glass-sheathed modernism makes Sobek's design a landmark in the history of green architecture.

Finally, in Asia and Australia we unearthed designs that offer a range of inventive responses to local and regional conditions. In the shadow of the Great Wall, about 50 miles north of Beijing, Japanese architect Kengo Kuma turned a hilly site into a stunning essay on the sculptural possibilities of bamboo, a highly sustainable material given how quickly and cheaply it can be grown. In Tasmania, a weekend house by the firm 1+2 Architecture touches down in its bushland setting with remarkable lightness and grace. In Japan, Shigeru Ban took an unusual request for a family residence with as little privacy as possible and produced the Naked House, an inexpensive and infinitely flexible design with a form that echoes the greenhouses that stand nearby.

Every one of these designs easily satisfied our primary goal: to find houses that are as ambitious architecturally as they are in terms of sustainability. While some are futuristic and others charmingly low-tech, the majority mix new eco-friendly strategies with vernacular ones. Taken as a group, these homes suggest that while there is no particular template that green houses must adhere to, there is also no rule stating that they can't have plenty of style or aim for the highest aesthetic plane.

In other words, green architecture is finally ready for its close-up.

Standards and Practices

So what does it mean, exactly, to say that a house is "green"? It is difficult to define the term with complete precision. For starters, we like the straightforward suggestion from the David and Lucile Packard Foundation that "any building that has significantly lower negative environmental impacts than traditional buildings" qualifies as green.[1] More broadly, the key, most experts agree, is a flexible and holistic approach that involves making careful, ecologically conscious decisions at every point in the planning, design, and construction processes while keeping in mind that the ideal solution may not always be evident. An architect or would-be homeowner deciding, for instance,

between a kind of roofing material created in an environmentally wasteful manner but available locally and an eco-friendly variety that has to be trucked in from 2,500 miles away will not be helped much by a universal green design checklist. In general, though, there are steady guidelines to be followed and priorities to be kept in mind. Residential designs that aim for authentic greenness should, at the very least, be:

- as small as possible, for a house that uses every sustainable technique under the sun will not be as kind to the Earth as practically any house half its size;
- positioned to take advantage of winter sun and summer shade, and to minimize damage to the plants, animals, soil, etc. already there;
- located as close to public transportation, workplaces, schools, and/or shopping as realistically possible.

Those are the basics; importantly, none of them need add any cost to the construction of a new home (save for the potentially higher prices of land in or near a city). Indeed, following the first rule will necessarily lead to lower building costs.

Beyond that, greenness is generally a question of two issues—energy efficiency and the eco-friendliness of a building's materials—along with a broader sense of how a new house or apartment building ties into its local, regional, and global context. Often, these concerns are intertwined, but in general architects committed to sustainability will employ many (and in rare cases all) of the following:

- recycled materials and even existing foundations or building shells;
- wood from stocks that are sustainably managed;
- materials that are low in embodied energy— that is, the energy required to extract and produce them as well as to deliver them to a building site;
- natural materials, such as bamboo, that can be easily replenished;
- efficient lighting systems that take advantage of daylight to reduce electricity needs or include sensors and timers that shut off lights when they are not in use;
- water systems that collect rainwater or treat so-called gray water (from sinks and showers) so that it can be reused for gardens or toilets;
- strategies to ensure that a house will have a long life because it is comfortable to spend time in, architecturally significant, or adaptable to future uses;

Great (Bamboo) Wall, by Kengo Kuma.

1 The David and Lucile Packard Foundation, Building for Sustainability Report, October 2002, 9.

- insulation, glass, and facades that are energy-efficient and that promote cooling by natural ventilation instead of by air-conditioning;
- features that take advantage of the sun's rays, either passively, using thermal massing and high-efficiency glass, or actively through photovoltaic panels, to turn sunlight into electricity;
- interior materials and finishes, from carpets to paints, that minimize chemical emissions and promote good air quality.

After much thought and discussion with various leaders in the field, we decided to use an admittedly flexible definition of sustainability in this book. True sustainability, of course, means a house that produces as much energy as it consumes. More than a few of the houses here would fail to qualify as green by that standard. For architects and clients alike, it is not always realistic to expect perfection. The point is to make careful, informed choices from selecting a site to picking out the cabinetry. Along with the idea that green houses are now being produced by many of the world's most talented architects, what we are interested in communicating here is the notion that sustainability is not exotic or better left to specialists, but based in the kind of common sense that is comprehensible for any potential home-builder—or home-buyer, for that matter.

It is true that building a new house of any kind will rarely be a positive environmental gesture. But no matter how ecologically progressive our society becomes, demand for new housing is not going to dry up anytime soon. About 1.5 million single-family homes went up in the United States in 2003 alone, according to the National Association of Home Builders[2]—the vast majority of them, sadly, following not a single green design principle. But more and more, architects are finding ways to reduce the margin between the amount of resources consumed in the construction and operation of a house and those saved or replenished. Indeed, by combining ancient techniques with the latest in super-efficient mechanical systems and materials, the designers of the houses we've documented here are managing to make that margin astonishingly small.

A Very Short History

Perhaps the most important thing to say about the origins of sustainable residential designs is that they lie in ageless vernacular architecture, the kind of construction that was practiced for most of human history and continues to be practiced in what we in the West call the Third World. This approach relies on simple, renewable, and naturally insulating materials (such as adobe) and passive strategies like siting, thick walls, and natural ventilation to keep houses cool in summer and retain heat in winter. Roughly one-third of the world's population continues to live in such architecture. The lessons it offers for building environmentally responsible and energy-efficient housing remain as valuable and easy to copy as ever.

In a stylistic sense, to oversimplify at least a little, Western architecture has been drifting away from those traditions since the Greeks. Still, the divorce between architecture and the environment was not really finalized until the beginning of the twentieth century, when the modernists' love affair with new industrial technologies, from the elevator to steel-frame construction, produced an architecture that did its best to exist apart from nature. Indeed, by the early decades of the twentieth century the ideal piece of residential architecture had become a rectilinear, pure-white box set off in a field. The modernist master Le Corbusier called his version "a machine for living," a building that gained its undeniable charisma precisely from the way it was everything that the field was not: hard where the field was soft, monochromatic instead of multihued, closed instead of open, its edges factory-cut instead of weather-softened.

The critique of modernist architecture as anti-green is by now a familiar one, and we think it has sometimes been overstated. It is worth pointing out, for example, that modernism began with the same kind of reform-minded ethos that now drives green architecture—and that some of the figures who helped inspire the sustainability movement, Buckminster Fuller prominently among them, were believers in modernism who hoped to harness technology to improve the lives of the average family. As Kevin Pratt, an architect and critic based in London, has pointed out, "Green design speaks to a yearning for the kind of totalizing aesthetic and ideological program the modernists embraced. [It] also shares with the modernist project the righteousness of a cause: improving the world through reform of its material culture."[3] In addition, a significant number of green landmarks over the last two decades have been designed by architects, like Britain's High Tech Group, whose approach and methodology grew directly from modernism.

Naked House, by Shigeru Ban.

2 National Association of Home Builders, "Monthly Housing Starts (2001–current)," at www.nahb.org.
3 Kevin Pratt, "Conserving Habitats," *Artforum*, February 2004, 62.

Pratt and other critics have gone so far as to predict that sustainability will be to the twenty-first century what modernism was to the twentieth—its dominant architectural movement.

Yet even we fans of modern architecture have to admit the wisdom—and the foresight—of the writers and architects who lined up to complain about its sometimes blindly universal approach, as well as, more generally, the dehumanizing effects of rapid industrialization. These critics included William Morris and John Ruskin in England and, later, Frank Lloyd Wright and Jane Jacobs in the United States—a diverse group, to be sure, writing across nearly a century. But what they all expressed was a deep anxiety about the ways in which architecture was turning away from the same basic lessons of the profession, passed down from architect to architect and amateur builder to amateur builder, that make up the fundamentals of green design—lessons about human scale and how buildings relate to their natural surroundings and to organic forms that can be appreciated day to day, season to season, and year to year. Their critiques became particularly persuasive in the 1960s, as modernism came to seduce urban planners and big-city mayors as powerfully as it had private clients.

What finally allowed such misgivings to coalesce into a proper movement was the realization during the second half of the twentieth century that human activity was beginning to put the planet itself in peril. This realization prompted—and was prompted by—many scientific and political milestones, from Rachel Carson's seminal book *Silent Spring* in 1962 to the inaugural Earth Day in 1970 to assessments like the Club of Rome's 1972 book *The Limits to Growth*, which predicted, all too accurately, that humans would soon begin using the Earth's resources more quickly than they could be replenished. It was the oil crisis of the mid-1970s, though, that produced real environmental urgency in Western societies for the first time. All of a sudden, every human activity that used up more natural resources than could be replaced became suspect. What this crisis meant for architecture was that the dismay with hard-edged, mechanistic designs expressed by Ruskin, Wright, and their heirs could be regarded as more than mere aesthetic dissatisfaction. It was no longer a simple architectural argument about whether one preferred a building dripping with ornament or a blank facade. The question became whether those responsible for putting up buildings would

help address the increasingly unstable, unhealthy relationship between human civilization and the natural world.

By the 1980s, the movement finally had a name for its goal: sustainability. The term was brought into popular use by the Brundtland Report, a 1987 United Nations document that defined sustainable development as meeting "the needs of the present without compromising the ability of future generations to meet their own."[4] The concept provided architects with a sense of membership in an important larger effort, a way of defining precisely what they hoped to accomplish with their solar panels and walls made from recycled tires.

Even so, it took a while before the concept of sustainability merged vernacular elements with energy-efficient building practices to create what we now call green architecture. As a formal effort, the movement is younger than you might guess. As early as 1981 there were books like Robert Brown Butler's *The Ecological House* and proto-green developments like Davis, California's Village Homes, but they were isolated efforts that predated any broad sense of eco-friendly architecture. Indeed, *The Green Reader*, a collection of essays published in 1991 that addressed sustainability in a wide variety of fields, did not mention architecture at all. But certainly by that year and soon after there were networks of architects who had begun to organize their practices around an ecologically sensitive approach to construction. The American Institute of Architects created its Committee on the Environment in 1992. The U.S. Green Building Council, a nonprofit association whose members include architects, developers, and builders, was founded in 1993. The first comprehensive books on the subject, such as Michael J. Crosbie's *Green Architecture: A Guide to Sustainable Design*, began appearing in bookstores over the following few years, and by the end of the millennium the term "green architecture" had seeped into the popular discourse.

A Movement's Priorities

As green architecture developed throughout the 1980s and 1990s, its leaders tended to pay little, if any, attention to the high-design or academic corners of the architecture world. Instead, they rather stubbornly saw green design's priorities as higher-minded or simply more pressing than style or theory. They were determined to pay most of their attention (and perhaps quite rightly, given

Walla Womba Guest House, by 1+2 Architecture.

4 Thabo Mbeki, et al., "We Can Do This Work Together," *International Herald Tribune*, 28 August 2002.

who makes the decisions about how and where to build, especially in the United States) to convincing corporate America that green design should be a mainstream rather than a marginal or eccentric pursuit.

In that battle they have made tremendous and undeniable progress. Sustainability advocates can finally say with confidence that the goals of green design have been embraced by a wide public. That public may be even wider than we suspect: though they do not advertise this fact, even George W. Bush and his wife Laura have become patrons of green architecture. Their ranch house in Crawford, Texas, designed by Austin architect David Heymann and finished the same year Bush became President, has a number of sustainable features, including a system for recycling household water.[5]

The Green Building Council's sustainable rating system for new buildings—known by its acronym LEED, for Leadership in Energy and Environmental Design—has achieved wide cultural currency since its formal introduction in 2000. It is not unusual now even for large corporate clients to push their architects to achieve a LEED rating because they know the public equates those standards with environmental responsibility. More than 1,000 buildings in the U.S. have earned LEED certification or are seeking it—roughly 5 percent of all commercial construction in this country, with that proportion surely bound to increase each year. (Already, roughly one in five institutional and government buildings are being built to LEED standards.) A LEED program for commercial interiors was launched in 2004, and one for residential architecture in 2005.

One of the biggest deterrents to sustainable building has been the perception of added expense. According to a study commissioned by the state of California, LEED buildings cost an average of $4 more per square foot than typical construction.[6] But over twenty years, the study suggests, "they would generate savings of $48.87 a square foot (in current dollars) for standard- and silver-certified buildings, and $67.31 for gold- and platinum-certified buildings."[7] To be fair, there is some guesswork involved in these projections; they rely on assumptions that green buildings will not only have lower operating costs than traditional ones but also that they will be more comfortable to work in, thereby increasing employee productivity.

Meanwhile, technological and manufacturing advances have made many green design features cheaper and easier to obtain than they had been. Solar panels designed to generate electricity, for example, cost about $100 per watt in the mid-1970s; they now sell for less than $3 per watt, and the price is continuing to fall.[8] And new eco-friendly building materials appear on what seems a daily basis. Consider PV-TV, an inventive version of the solar panel developed in Japan. It can be used on the facade of a building in three ways at once: as a solar collector to generate electricity, as a transparent pane to allow sunlight into the interior, and as a screen to display video images.[9]

As green architecture was gaining supporters in the political and commercial spheres, however, it was utterly failing to win them in the aesthetic realm. Sustainable building became associated in the public imagination with earnest, uninspired designs that put environmental concerns far ahead of artistic ones, creating what some critics dubbed the curse of "eco-banality." If in recent years you asked the average reader of an architecture or home design magazine, say, to close her eyes and describe what came to mind at the mention of "green design" or "eco-architecture," she probably would have mentioned a sagging sod roof or a corporate office building with some energy-efficient features but little to recommend it architecturally.

Those architects most often covered in the design and popular press, especially academics and self-styled members of the avant-garde, wasted few opportunities to denigrate sustainable design. For them, as one writer put it, green architecture had "no edge, no buzz, no style." It was not only "populated by the self-righteous and the badly dressed" but "a haven for the untalented, where ethics replace aesthetics and get away with it."[10] The architect Peter Eisenman, long a member of the architectural vanguard, had this to say on the subject as late as 2001: "To talk to me about sustainability is like talking to me about giving birth. Am I against giving birth? No. But would I like to spend my time doing it? Not really. I'd rather go to a baseball game."[11]

There have been many explanations put forth about why so many of the most famous architects in the world spent the last several years fleeing sustainability as quickly as their Prada-clad feet could carry them. Harrison Fraker, dean of the College of Environmental Design at the University of California at Berkeley, suggests that they have feared allowing anyone to pull back the curtain on the mystique that maintains any kind of

5 Andrew Blum, "George W. Bush Builds his Dream House," *The New Yorker*, 24 July 2000, 27.
6 Barnaby J. Feder, "Environmentally Conscious Developers Try to Turn Green into Platinum," *The New York Times*, 25 August 2004.
7 Ibid.
8 Barnaby J. Feder, "A Different Era for Alternative Energy," *The New York Times*, 29 May 2004.
9 Eliza Barclay, "PV-TV: A Multifunctional, Eco-Friendly Building Material," *Metropolis*, 27 July 2004, online edition, at www.metropolismag.com.
10 Susannah Hagan, "Five Reasons to Adopt Environmental Design," *Harvard Design Magazine*, Spring/Summer 2003, 5.
11 Quoted in Christopher Hawthorne, "The Case for a Green Aesthetic," *Metropolis*, October 2001, 113.

celebrity. Even those famous architects who design environmentally conscious buildings—Fraker cites the highly regarded Swiss duo Herzog & de Meuron as an example—are weary of the "green designer" label. "They worry that talking about green design will make environmentalism the center of their public reputation,"[12] he argues. And that, in turn, might diminish their appeal.

A different assessment comes from Susannah Hagan, who runs a master's program in sustainability at the University of East London and has written extensively on the subject. For her, the traditional distance between the avant-garde and green design has had more to do with the former's preoccupation with theory over material. Though the sustainability movement rests on a philosophical foundation made up of figures as diverse as John Muir, Henry David Thoreau, Edward Abbey, and Rachel Carson, on a day-to-day level the practice of green architecture has more to do with hands-on, practical considerations than it does with deep thinking or dazzling theory. In the theoretical wing of the architecture profession, Hagan senses what she calls "a sometimes explicit, sometimes subliminal resistance to architecture-as-matter."[13] And for star architects, their celebrity kept aloft by buzz and mystery, matter can seem dangerously close to mundane.

The Damage Done

Those architects' complaints about green design's lack of style, of course, were the design-world equivalent of fiddling while Rome burned. Indeed, for anyone who hasn't heard them before, the statistics on the amount of damage that the building industries do to the environment can be staggering. By one recent measure, buildings use 48 percent of all the energy consumed in the United States each year and are responsible for about half of American greenhouse gas emissions, which drive global warming.[14] More than one third of the material clogging U.S. landfills is produced by the construction and demolition of buildings.[15] Worldwide, the numbers are not quite so bad but still drastically worse than they ought to be, and soaring population growth and rapid industrialization and urbanization in China, India, and elsewhere promises to wipe out the environmental progress being made in both the developed and developing world. Indeed, China now ranks second in the world, behind only the United States, as an emitter of greenhouse gases and is likely to take over the top spot on that dubious list within the next decade.[16] And without a drastic

global commitment to green architecture, the situation promises to get much worse. According to William Clark, a professor at Harvard's Kennedy School of Government, "Over the next twenty to forty years, by any of the prevailing demographic calculations, there will be more urban built environment created than in all prior history."[17]

Much of the environmental damage is the indirect result, many green design advocates say, of an architecture that has increasingly alienated its users from the natural world. "Our culture has adopted a design stratagem that essentially says that if brute force or massive amounts of energy don't work, you're not using enough of it," says the architect William McDonough, among the best-known practitioners of sustainable architecture.

We made glass buildings that are more about buildings than they are about people.... The hope that glass would connect us to the outdoors was completely stultified by making the buildings sealed. We have created stress in people because we are meant to be connected with the outdoors, but instead we are trapped....People are sensing how horrifying it can be to be trapped indoors, especially with the thousands upon thousands of chemicals that are being used to make things today.[18]

Green design experts have pointed out that most contemporary architecture is connected to globalization of the most destructive order. "Phillipine forests are clear-cut for plywood used to build offices in Japan," notes the Rocky Mountain Institute's *Primer on Sustainable Building*.

Homes in Southern California are framed with old-growth lumber from Washington and powered by burning coal strip-mined from Navajo sacred lands in Arizona. Ultimately, the costs of poor design are borne not solely by a building's owner and those who work and live there, but by everyone.[19]

In the face of such statistics, it is easy to despair about the possibility of a turnaround, especially one led by architecture—and, more specifically, by residential architecture. After all, the number of private homes designed by architects each year around the world is tiny compared to the many buildings, from housing developments to office parks, that are constructed without the benefit of a design professional. What's more, those designed by the architects on the cutting edge of the profession would seem to have little direct

12 Ibid, 123.
13 Hagan, "Five Reasons," 11.
14 Christopher Hawthorne, "Turning Down the Global Thermostat," *Metropolis*, October 2003, 104.
15 Hawthorne, "The Case for a Green Aesthetic," 113.
16 "Climate Change: The Big Emitters," BBC News, 23 July 2004, online edition, at http://news.bbc.co.uk.
17 William Clark, "What Can We Do?" *Harvard Design Magazine*, Spring/Summer 2003, 58.
18 William McDonough, "Design, Ecology, Ethics, and the Making of Things," *Earth Island Journal*, Spring 1996, online edition, at www.earthisland.org/eijournal.
19 Dianna Lopez Barnett, et al., *Primer on Sustainable Design* (Snowmass, Colorado: Rocky Mountain Institute, 1995), 2.

Charlotte Residence, by William McDonough + Partners.

20 Quoted in Calvin Tomkins, "The Piano Principle," *The New Yorker*, 22 August 1994, 63.

21 Elizabeth Wilhide, *Eco: An Essential Sourcebook for Environmentally Friendly Design and Decoration* (New York: Rizzoli, 2003), 8.

22 Danny Hakim, "A Shade of Green: SUV's Try to Soften Image," *The New York Times*, 16 February 2004.

23 Hawthorne, "Turning Down the Global Thermostat," 104.

24 Hawthorne, "The Case for a Green Aesthetic," 113.

connection to the kind of suburban tract houses produced on a massive scale.

But architecture is a field, like fashion, where style, and even avant-garde style, matters more and more and is separated from the man on the street less and less with each passing year. Architects and builders alike—even those without fancy reputations—read the architecture and design press as surely as merchandisers for Target or Macy's follow what is on the runway in Milan or Paris. Since the 1997 opening of Frank Gehry's branch of the Guggenheim Museum in Bilbao, Spain, there has been a much-touted explosion of interest in design and architecture, and new connections have been forged between high-design architecture and the public at large. Even before it opened in 2003 in downtown Los Angeles, Gehry's Walt Disney Concert Hall was appearing in car ads in glossy magazines—surely proof, if any were still needed, that contemporary architecture is no longer estranged from popular culture.

Meanwhile, the number of well-known or avant-garde architects whose firms have been pursuing sustainable design in good faith has been growing. This group now includes such luminaries as Renzo Piano, Sir Norman Foster, Glenn Murcutt, and Herzog & de Meuron, all of whom have won the Pritzker Prize, architecture's version of the Nobel. Santiago Calatrava, designer of the critically acclaimed new transit hub for the World Trade Center site in lower Manhattan, lent his skills to a progressive sustainable neighborhood in Malmo, Sweden. What all of this means for the green design movement is simple: not only do architects have a celebrity status that they did not possess a decade ago, but even their experimental work has become part of mainstream culture. The fact that many famous architects are turning to green architecture suggests sustainability will gain exposure, in the media and elsewhere, that it might not receive otherwise.

It is also encouraging that technological progress, so long the enemy of the natural world, is increasingly being put in the service of saving and restoring nature—and that this new partnership is producing some of its most significant dividends in the realm of architecture, where modeling programs, to pick one example, now help designers measure the efficiency of their buildings with remarkable accuracy while they are still on the computer screen. As a result, green architects of all kinds are ditching their old reputation as regressive Luddites who were content to labor in isolation from cultural—and

architectural—developments. "At the beginning of the [twentieth] century, technology was like a big train breaking everything, a killing machine," Piano has said. "It was really an adversary to nature. But today you can begin to see that technology and nature are not so far apart."[20]

To be sure, there is no shortage in today's world of threats and sources of anxiety, from terrorism to emerging strains of disease. But as the author Elizabeth Wilhide points out in her recent book *Eco*, "Of all the dangers that threaten our world, damage to the environment is one menace we can all do something about."[21] And it makes better sense than we may realize to begin that effort with architecture. Though the construction industry, as we've seen, does more damage to the environment than any other single sector of society, it somehow continues to escape the sort of public scrutiny or scorn that greets other polluters. Why, for example, does the S.U.V. continue to qualify as the bête-noire of environmental advocates, as *The New York Times* recently put it,[22] when the building trades do about six times more damage than automobiles in terms of energy consumption and carbon dioxide emissions?[23]

If we began to look at the damage that is done by the buildings where we work, play, and live, we might find a more appropriate place to attach our worry and begin to do the slow, persistent work of turning the environmental situation around. Indeed, it is precisely because American homes and other buildings are so wasteful of energy that they represent such a tremendous potential for newfound savings. Just to pick one example of inefficiency, every year $16 billion worth of energy in the form of heated or cooled air escapes through cracks and holes in residential buildings in the United States alone.[24] Even if we are not homeowners, our residence remains the one place where we control the institutional behavior, as it were. And for those of us lucky enough not just to buy but to build our own homes, the level of control shoots way up. Home is where green architecture begins—or at least where it ought to.

Cities have been around for more

than six thousand years, drawing successive waves of new residents with their blend of commerce, culture, energy, and opportunity. The first city to surpass a population of one million was Baghdad, thirteen centuries ago. London topped five million in 1825; New York exceeded ten million a hundred years later. The metropolitan area around Tokyo surpassed twenty million in 1965 and is now closing in on thirty.

At the start of the twentieth century, there were sixteen cities with one million inhabitants; by the end of it, there were nearly four hundred. Today's "mega-" or "hypercities" have become choked with people: Bombay, São Paulo, Mexico City, Los Angeles, Shanghai, and Buenos Aires all have populations in excess of ten million. For the first time in human history, more people live in cities than outside of them.

For a long time, cities had a horrible reputation when it came to the environment. They were thought to be concrete jungles where residents were cut off from grass, trees, and fresh air and lived out of ecological balance. Some of that reputation is deserved: cities today consume more than 75 percent of the world's resources, although they take up a mere 2 percent of its land surface. But recently a more complex assessment of the relationship between urbanism and sustainability has emerged. First, cities have become more livable, thanks to falling crime rates and increased attention to issues like air quality. Second, cities are inherently dense, and density can greatly reduce a society's overall drain on natural resources. An apartment dweller who occupies less than 1,000 square feet, has no lawn to water, shares a heating system with his fellow tenants, and uses public transportation is far kinder to the environment than his counterpart in the suburbs who drives everywhere and lives in a single-family house on its own landscaped plot.

The most successful green projects in cities are small and moderately dense, such as apartments clustered in structures of less than six stories. But low-impact materials and technologies are also increasingly common in residential high-rises, which take advantage of green construction methods developed for commercial buildings. Builders have made great strides in reducing environmental impact by using harvested lumber and recycled materials, the installation of non-toxic and energy-efficient insulation systems, and the selection of building sites that take maximum advantage of solar and wind power as well as access to public transportation. It is worth noting that one of the most popular types of urban construction—converting industrial buildings into residential properties—is intrinsically green. Recycling and renewing old structures are among the best ways to minimize waste and preserve resources.

Cities large and small have deployed successful programs to halt sprawl with the help of tax breaks and other incentives for inner-city development. Some have begun to redevelop their waterfront districts into cultural and residential zones, renovating their existing stock of buildings in the process. Planners are also narrowing commuting distances between commercial and residential areas and designing ever more sophisticated systems of transportation within residential developments. Many architects and planners are thinking more broadly about the environmental impact of their building methods, for example, by including transportation costs in their calculations about the sustainability of different materials. With its recyclable resources, existing infrastructure, and density of suppliers, the city turns out to be a potentially eco-friendly site for home construction.

Urban construction offers numerous opportunities for securing buildings against energy loss. Many structures, especially in dense urban cores, are erected between existing buildings and therefore exposed to the elements on only two sides. And, increasingly, cities are turning building tops into "eco-roofs," planted with sod or native grasses, which help lower a structure's energy use by promoting natural evaporation in summer and providing insulation in winter. Green roofs are appearing at a time when we are realizing that cities resemble nature more closely than we once admitted—and vice versa. As Jane Jacobs wrote in a 2004 article for *The New York Times Magazine*, "In its need for variety and acceptance of randomness, a flourishing natural ecosystem is more like a city than like a plantation. Perhaps it will be the city that reawakens our understanding and appreciation of nature, in all its teeming, unpredictable complexity."

P.A.R.A.S.I.T.E. PROJECT

LOCATION
Rotterdam, the Netherlands

ARCHITECTURAL FIRM
Korteknie Stuhlmacher Architecten

DESIGNERS
**Rien Korteknie and
Mechthild Stuhlmacher**

YEAR
2001

At first glance, it's hard to tell what the angular building, painted a shade of light green bordering on chartreuse, is doing attached to the roof of a warehouse near the Maas River in Rotterdam. It looks as though it could be a sculpture or temporary artwork, or a piece of architecture produced as a lark. Actually, the building is a prototype for an entirely new kind of urban housing, one that mixes pragmatism and sustainability with a design sensibility that is far more sophisticated than it initially appears to be.

← The first P.A.R.A.S.I.T.E. project, a prototype for a sustainable, opportunistic kind of urban housing, is attached to a stairwell atop a renovated warehouse in the Dutch city of Rotterdam.

This is the P.A.R.A.S.I.T.E. project, designed by a pair of Dutch architects named Rien Korteknie and Mechthild Stuhlmacher. It is the first realized project in a series of experimental small houses developed to coincide with Rotterdam's designation as the European Cultural Capital in 2001. The idea was to enlist young architects to design prototypes for housing that make parasitic use of existing urban infrastructure. As the program's materials put it, the sites for these projects are meant to be "all kinds of urban locations that are usually regarded as being unsuitable for permanent inhabitation, such as former industrial sites, the flat roofs of existing buildings, locations on the water," or other "disused" spots in the contemporary city. The acronym P.A.R.A.S.I.T.E. stands for Prototype for Advanced Ready-made Amphibious Small-scale Individual Temporary Ecological dwelling.

The building site for Korteknie and Stuhlmacher's P.A.R.A.S.I.T.E. project is the top of a warehouse in Rotterdam called Las Palmas, which has been renovated and now serves as an exhibition space for art shows, design exhibitions, and other events. Their prototype is designed to explore the potential of new architectural systems that combine sustainability and prefabrication. In this case, the architects used large, laminated panels called LenoTec that are made of European waste wood and can be used for walls, floors, and even roofs. The panels are load-bearing and insulating at the same time, though in some climates additional insulation may be needed.

The project's most sustainable feature is the way it relates to the city. The structure suggests a type of housing that would take advantage of existing (and often underused) water and heating systems in old industrial buildings. It would also tie directly into urban transportation systems and add to the density of European cities, cutting back the need for resource-draining suburban sprawl. Indeed, the design of this Rotterdam P.A.R.A.S.I.T.E. offers something of a critique, the architects say, of housing policy in the Netherlands, a country that has struggled to control development in the suburban areas between its biggest cities. What they propose is a stylish new kind of urban infill, a type of city apartment that doesn't require an empty lot or the demolition of an existing building.

Korteknie and Stuhlmacher designed the house with advanced computer modeling software. They used the same program to run the milling machines in the LenoTec factory as they used to design the panels. The panels were trucked to the site and basic assembly was completed in just four days. The P.A.R.A.S.I.T.E., just under 1,000 square feet in total, was built for about $115 per square foot—less than half the average cost for architect-designed homes in the United States, which run roughly $250 per square foot and up.

From the outside, the building may look temporary and even fragile, but inside it feels surprisingly permanent and finished. The spaces are beautifully and intelligently proportioned and offer dramatic views of Rotterdam, including, most prominently, UN Studio's highly acclaimed Erasmus Bridge.

This attention to detail is also part of the architects' commentary on typical residential construction in the Netherlands, particularly in the suburbs; while some of the country's best-known architects have been hired to produce new suburban developments, they have tended

to lavish more care on the exterior architecture than on the interiors, making for complexes that look great in magazine spreads but don't always please their residents. The P.A.R.A.S.I.T.E. project is designed with different priorities. Though the house looks ad-hoc from the outside, most visitors given the opportunity to tour the interior make exactly the same pronouncement: they wouldn't mind living here themselves.

↑ Factory-built panels made of waste wood were shipped to the site and assembled on the roof of the warehouse before being raised into place.

→ A bird's-eye view of the finished house reveals its parasitic use of the infrastructure of the building underneath.

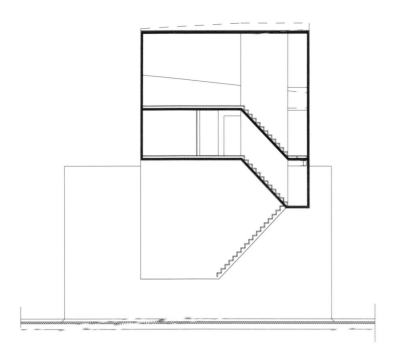

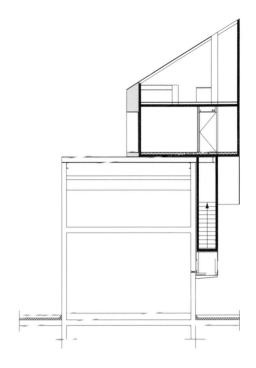

⬉ | ↑ Elevations illustrate how the house perches atop the existing building's stairwell.

↓ The floor plan shows interior stairs leading from a single room on the lower level to a living space and terrace upstairs.

← A long stair, bottom left, leads to two floors of interior space and a terrace. The rooms look unfinished but achieve a surprisingly sophisticated feel.

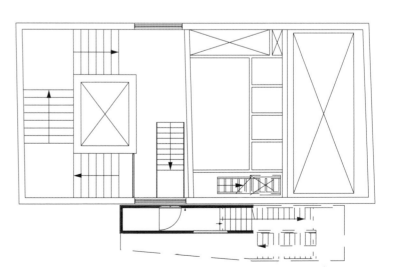

156 READE STREET

LOCATION
New York, New York

ARCHITECTURAL FIRM
Studio Petrarca

DESIGNER
John Petrarca

YEAR
2001

It is easy to see why hurried Manhattanites might overlook the architectural uniqueness of 156 Reade Street. While the six-story Tribeca townhouse boasts a striking glass-and-steel facade, its scale and ground-floor fenestration intentionally echo the neighborhood's historic cast-iron loft buildings. But even slow-paced, inquisitive pedestrians and architecture buffs will fail to notice the most astonishing feature of the structure, since it is hidden 1,100 feet underground.

← Prefabricated in a local bridge-building shop, the south-facing steel facade of John Petrarca's Tribeca townhouse was assembled on the street and then lifted into place in what he described as an "urban adaptation of a barn raising."

↑ The fire-engine red stairwell features a stainless-steel mesh drape and glass treads.

Standing on a small, shallow lot, only 25 feet wide, the building is heated and cooled with a geothermal pump that is nearly as deep as the Empire State Building is tall. The water under New York City has a constant temperature of 55 degrees. With a network of heat exchangers and chillers, the pump system capitalizes on the earth's own heat, using up to 75 percent less energy than conventional heating systems because of the relatively small differential between the 55-degree water temperature and a comfortable room temperature. The system also produces no air pollution and, over time, saves on costs. Each floor in the house has its own thermostat, allowing for targeted climate control, which further reduces energy demand. In the summer, the pump operates in reverse, sucking heat out of the house and circulating cool water.

The geothermal pump is just one of several environmentally progressive features that the late architect John Petrarca integrated into the home and office he designed for himself and his family. (Sadly, he only lived in it briefly before succumbing to lung cancer in 2003, at the age of 51.) According to Roberta Woelfling, who was an associate of Petrarca's while he was working on the project, "his goal was to make the house as environmentally sensitive to its inhabitants as it would be to the Earth." All the interior and exterior materials—from the steel of the facade to the concrete walls and natural wood finishes—were chosen for their non-toxic and low-impact properties. The house features a ventilation system that provides an unusually high level of filtration and fresh air, free of pollen, mold, and particulate. Neither the cabinetry nor the wood flooring contains formaldehyde, and anything with vinyl or varnish was strictly off-limits. Petrarca was "always looking for green sources, local sources, and for ways to conserve fuel and electricity," Woelfling says.

Petrarca, who became interested in finding creative solutions to local problems during a stint in the Peace Corps after college, devised an environmentally sensitive construction protocol. For the poured concrete walls, he used Styrofoam forms to raise energy efficiency and conserve material. The foam provides extra insulation and, unlike standard wood forms, which are typically discarded, it stays in place and becomes part of the structure itself. The 20-ton steel facade was prefabricated—another environmentally efficient solution—by a New Jersey bridge-building shop and assembled on-site in Tribeca.

An open-plan living area on the fourth floor takes advantage of the natural light flowing in through the large, south-facing windows. Beneath the family room's 22-foot-high ceiling, richly marbled walnut paneling (which Petrarca found through a service that re-purposes trees people have cut down for one reason or another) warms up the living area. That space is further distinguished by a Chinese quartzite stone fireplace wall and radiant-heated limestone floors. A fifth-floor mezzanine hanging over the living room offers desk space and a lounge from which to admire the sweeping views of lower Manhattan and the Hudson River. Above it is the penthouse guest room, which includes a balcony and kitchenette. The master bedroom suite encompasses the entire third floor and incorporates a split-faced marble master bath. The second floor, with two bedrooms and a playroom, is the children's realm. On the ground floor is a generous storage space and what Petrarca's widow, Sarah Bartlett, calls "the engine room," where the controls for the pump and its monitoring devices are housed.

←← The ground-floor entryway is paneled in reclaimed walnut and incorporates two cast-iron columns from the site's original building.

← On the fifth-floor mezzanine, large south- and west-facing windows offer sweeping views.

↙↙ The living room, which extends off the dining area, has a 22-foot–high walnut-paneled ceiling, a limestone floor, and a Chinese quartzite fireplace surround.

↙ Below the mezzanine, the fourth-floor open-plan kitchen and dining area are set off by a wall of formaldehyde-free Bulthaup cabinets.

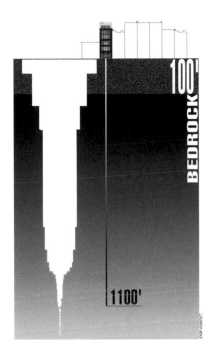

↑ A geothermal pump that heats and cools the building uses water raised from 1,100 feet beneath Manhattan, roughly the height of the Empire State Building.

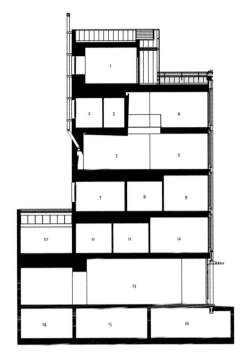

Section
1 Penthouse/guest
2 Guest bathroom
3 Pantry/laundry
4 Study
5 Living room
6 Kitchen/dining
7 Master bathroom
8 Dressing room
9 Master bedroom
10 Playroom
11 Bathroom
12 Kid's bedroom
13 Home office
14 Conference room
15 Storage
16 Workshop

A dramatic steel-and-glass staircase, painted fire-engine red and capped by a large skylight, knits together the floors of the 6,500-square-foot building. From the top of the stairwell Petrarca draped one long swath of stainless-steel mesh, which cascades all the way down to the basement level in lieu of a handrail. The result is a visually dramatic — and fireproof — centerpiece to the highly trafficked staircase. (The house, which was designed so that it could be easily converted into separate apartments, also includes a private elevator.)

For Bartlett, who has vivid memories of the three noisy days it took to drill for the pump, the house has become a technological teaching tool since her husband's death. "I never expected to be living here without him, but now that I am, I've learned a lot about how all the systems work. Luckily, John labeled everything and left extensive documentation — he was obsessive that way," she says. "At first it all seemed a bit overwhelming — I had no clue about things like monitoring the chillers — and I thought about leaving. But how could I go? My kids get such a psychic benefit from being here. I know it's a good place to live."

COLORADO COURT

ARCHITECTURAL FIRM
Pugh + Scarpa Architecture

DESIGNER
Angela Brooks

LOCATION
Santa Monica, California

YEAR
2002

The most advanced sustainable projects tend to serve high-end clients, whether they are wealthy, far-sighted individuals willing to pay extra to push the boundaries of green design or deep-pocketed companies banking on the long-term benefits and positive publicity that come along with environmentally efficient architecture. Very few commercial clients who are scrambling to make ends meet decide to invest aggressively in sustainable design. And most landlords are not about to install solar panels or recycled water systems just so they can help lower their tenants' utility bills. But at the corner of Fifth Street and Colorado Avenue in Santa Monica stands a monument to a different kind of green thinking, its grid of 199 blue solar panels reflecting the bright Southern California sunshine. Colorado Court, a five-story, forty-four–unit apartment complex that welcomed its first tenants in early 2003, is the first large residential complex in the United States to combine advanced sustainability with low-income housing. It was named one of the Top Ten Green Projects of 2003 by the American Institute of Architects.

← The forty-four–unit Colorado Court complex is covered with deep blue photovoltaic panels and graced by open-air walkways that allow residents to enjoy breezes from the nearby Pacific Ocean.

Designed by the Santa Monica firm Pugh + Scarpa, Colorado Court produces enough energy to satisfy 92 percent of its power needs. And it includes a list of sustainable features as long as any building in America, from age-old gestures like natural ventilation to recycled materials. It also makes an effort to fight sprawl by keeping its low-income tenants within walking or biking distance of their jobs and shopping.

There is no doubt that residents of Santa Monica are finding themselves squeezed when it comes to affording a place to live. In the years between 1996 and 2001, according to one estimate, the average cost of a two-bedroom rental in San Monica nearly doubled, jumping from $818 per month to more than $1,500. During the same period, the median value of a house in the city rose by 44 percent.

The apartments in Colorado Court offer a much-needed alternative. The single-residency studio apartments, though small at 300 to 375 square feet, are a bargain by the city's standards, renting for around $350 per month. Furthermore, tenants pay virtually no utility bills. As the architects explain in a description of the project they prepared for the U.S. Department of Energy, Colorado Court's aim is to "maintain socioeconomic diversity in this highly desirable beach community [with] an accelerating cost of living."

Pugh + Scarpa partner Angela Brooks suggests that low-income tenants are precisely the kind of residents whom green architecture ought to be serving—particularly in California, where the utility markets have been prone to huge price upswings in recent years. "This group of people is the least able to pay for things like water and power," she says. "When utility bills go up, it hurts them much more than others."

Needless to say, rental revenues are not enough to pay the mortgage. The building's total budget of $4.7 million—not including the land it sits on, which was donated by the city—was funded by a complicated mixture of sources and coordinated by its developer, the nonprofit Community Corporation of Santa Monica. Direct grants were combined with tax breaks to get the building off the ground. The architects estimate that the green features added about $14,000 to the cost of each unit, or just over $600,000 in total.

From the beginning, it was important to the architects, who work in the modernist vein, that the building have some architectural panache. Though they bemoan some of the "rather primitive" ways in which the contractor translated their design into three-dimensions, the building is nonetheless quite unusual among low-income projects for its clean, contemporary aesthetic and bold sense of color.

→ | →→ The 199 photovoltaic panels covering the facade (and portions of the roof) represent a rare effort to turn solar power into an aesthetic virtue. The 5-by-5–inch panels generate more than 90 percent of the building's electricity needs.

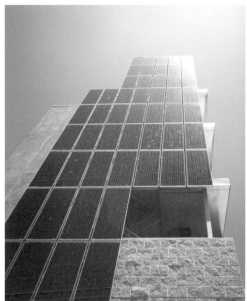 

← The building is w-shaped in plan, with two long wings at the perimeter and a shorter one in the middle.

In plan, Colorado Court is made of three arms—two long ones on the outside and a shorter one in the center—that reach out to catch the prevailing breezes, some of which come right off the nearby Pacific Ocean. In elevation, it has a precise, squared-off look, with outdoor hallways connecting the units on each floor. The indigo solar panels, comprised of 5-inch square receptors, make the building immediately recognizable even from a distance of a several hundred yards. Natural light, breezes, and 10-foot ceilings help the units feel open to the outside and less cramped than their square footage might suggest.

Brooks is upfront about the problems the architects and developer faced in trying to see the project through to completion with its sustainable elements intact. Dealing with the city and the local utility was especially tricky, she says, because each of those entities was simultaneously in charge of the regulatory process and also an investor in

the building. Sometimes the architects would meet with one city or utility official and be given positive news, only to have it revoked by a different official a few weeks later. Funding and approval for the gas-powered micro-turbine generator on the roof, designed to supplement the solar generation, were particularly tough to secure.

Looking back, Brooks says, "A lot of the hurdles we had to go through had nothing to do with the actual systems or materials themselves—those were relatively easy to figure out and deal with. But we had resistance from the utility company, the building department, subcontractors, the solar panel company and, surprisingly, our own engineers." In the end, though, the legacy of Colorado Court is not likely to be the difficulties that the architects faced in getting it built but rather how dramatically it has raised the bar for green projects of its size and degree of social consciousness.

VIIKKI

ARCHITECTURAL FIRM
Various architects

LOCATION
Helsinki, Finland

YEAR
Ongoing

The Viikki section of Helsinki is still several years away from completion, but it already ranks, easily, as the largest and most ambitious green housing development in the world. Located in the geographical center of the city and about five miles northeast of downtown, it includes approximately 5,000 units as of this writing, with about 8,000 to come. It is home to a satellite campus of the University of Helsinki and a biotechnology incubator, as well as public schools scattered throughout its streets. Eventually it will accommodate 6,000 jobs and 6,000 students to go along with its 13,000 residents. Theoretically, it will be possible for a child born to a family living there to go through primary, secondary, and university education, and then begin working within its confines, all without having to leave the neighborhood.

← Viikki's residential areas include townhouses by Finnish architect Kirsti Siven that open onto private gardens and gravel walking paths.

The project is essentially a proving ground for any number of green building strategies, from mixed-use development to innovative energy generation. The idea is to put sustainability to the test of actual construction and occupation and see what works and what doesn't, and then apply those lessons to building codes to control residential development throughout the country, particularly in publicly funded projects. There are a variety of approaches to renewable energy on view in Viikki, from wind turbines to several kinds of active solar collection. Rainwater is collected throughout and used for gardening, while gray-water systems recycle water from sinks and bathtubs for use elsewhere in the development.

The master plan for Viikki and its early housing blocks were selected via competition, beginning in 1998. Entries were judged on a thirty-four point scale in the following five categories: how well they limited 1) pollution and 2) the use of natural resources, how much they promoted 3) healthiness and 4) biodiversity, and 5) the extent to which they provided opportunities for residents to grow their own food. The general guidelines were slightly less strict but were still governed by sustainability at every turn: they required a 20 percent reduction in carbon dioxide emissions from building materials and pure water consumption, 10 percent less waste on building sites during construction, and a 20 percent cut in the average mixed refuse produced by each resident annually. The biggest savings are in the area of heating energy, where solar power, primarily, is helping reduce consumption by 60 percent per year. In addition, Viikki is closely tied to public transportation, reachable by several bus lines and by Helsinki's subway.

Walking around Viikki, it's easy to get a sense of those priorities in action. It's not just the solar panels shimmering on the facade of architect Reijo Jallinoja's eight-story apartment block near the main entrance but also the gardens full of fruits and vegetables that stretch between buildings; the sounds of children playing on schoolyards echoing throughout; and the fact that marshland and even grazing areas for livestock have been preserved in the midst of brand-new architecture, allowing for remarkably wide-open views—given Viikki's urban location—from some of the apartments.

As with any project of this size, the architecture in Viikki is a mixed bag. But at least a half-dozen of the development's apartment blocks stand out as models of aesthetic as well as sustainable excellence. These include Kirsti Siven's detached townhouses, completed in 2003, and a wood-and-glass mixed-use building by Mikko Bonsdorff that wouldn't look out of place in Portland or Seattle. Though Viikii remains little-known among architects and planners outside of Finland, it deserves to be an object of envy for the comprehensive, forward-looking way it treats urban growth. It aims to be nothing less than a fully self-contained, sustainable community, and is not far from reaching that ambitious goal.

← The Viikki development is one of the most ambitious experiments in sustainable architecture and urban planning in the world, with buildings designed to generate solar and wind power, direct rainwater to communal gardens, and preserve marshland—all in the geographical center of Finland's biggest city.

↓ Among the most impressive pieces of architecture is this design by Mikko Bonsdorff.

↓ The complex is a testing ground for a range of experiments in sustainability that includes schools, such as this one by ARK-house Architects, and incubators for various industries, along with a projected 13,000 residential units.

1310 EAST UNION STREET

ARCHITECTURAL FIRM
The Miller/Hull Partnership

DESIGNER
David Miller

LOCATION
Seattle, Washington

YEAR
2001

When former high-tech executive Liz Dunn decided to start a new career, she revisited her old dream of becoming an architect. After taking a few classes in architecture, urban planning, and real estate development at the University of Washington, she embarked on an ambitious project—a real estate venture that would blend high architectural aspirations with environmental responsibility. Already a committed environmental activist, she was particularly concerned about the cultural causes of environmental degradation, especially the tendency for successful executives like herself, for example, to commute to work daily from Disneyesque McMansions outside Seattle.

That's how she hit upon the idea of transit-oriented housing—a solution to the evil twins of suburban sprawl and gasoline emissions. She looked for a location that would be convenient to people who use mass transportation. The site she selected to develop, in the Pike/Pine neighborhood of Seattle's Capitol Hill, is within walking distance of a proposed light-rail station. One parking space in the eight-unit building's garage is reserved for use in Seattle's shared car program.

Dunn hired Miller/Hull to design the project. The award-winning architectural firm produces buildings characterized by "regional modernism"—a plainly modernist style that emphasizes closeness to nature through the use of exposed timber, large windows, fine detailing, eco-friendly materials, and other design solutions inspired by the northwestern landscape. The firm has a strong reputation for matching a building's structure with the particular climactic, physical, and cultural demands of its site.

Located on the site of a former sex shop, the 17,000-square-foot, five-story building features eight loft condominiums, from 600 to 1,700 square feet in size (the design allows any two units on each floor to be joined into a single, spacious apartment). Zoned for both residential and commercial occupancy, the project is a mid-rise, mixed-use building with large operable overhead doors and storefront windows at its base.

Essentially a 40-foot-wide glass box, the structure is held together by an exposed steel frame that features a prominent, brick-red diagonal x-bracing to protect against earthquakes. The north and south sides are fully glazed to allow for maximum sunlight. Low-emission coating and Argon gas–infused windows from Hartung Glass Industries enable the residents to enjoy plentiful natural light without losing much heat. Most units are double-height along the window walls, with bedrooms located on a mezzanine. The flexible interiors are designed in a chic, industrial style, detailed with exposed steel beams, corrugated metal decking at the ceilings, and smooth concrete floors that downplay the building's environmental agenda. When their wall-size aluminum-framed glass garage doors are rolled up, the loft-style interiors take on the feel of a covered terrace. Small balconies and a large rooftop garden provide additional outdoor access.

The 1310 East Union Street project is part of a growing trend that is luring suburbanites back to the city. The building also represents an effort on the part of the developer to bring some of the best European design ideas to the United States. For example, since the 3,200-square-foot parcel was too small to accommodate the eight parking spaces required by the number of housing units in the building, the architects installed hydraulic parking lifts that allow two medium-size cars—the space is intentionally too small for S.U.V.s—to be stacked vertically in a single space. Equally ingenious is the use of the roof as outdoor space. Configured as a series of decks and accessed by metal spiral staircases, the roof offers panoramic views of Puget Sound and the Olympic Mountains.

← The five-story, mixed-use loft building in Seattle's Pike/Pine area has a limited number of parking spaces and is within walking distance of a light-rail station.

← Designed for flexibility over time, most of the units are double-height with open mezzanines and can be partitioned with panels or furniture arrangements for use as work or living space as needed.

↙↙ | ↙ Honest, unfinished materials such as corrugated metal decking and concrete were used for interior finishes as well as for exterior cladding.

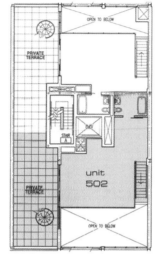

Mezzanine Floor Plan

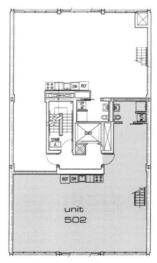

Main Floor Plan

↑ Large garage-style doors can be rolled back, allowing residents maximum exposure to fresh air and sunlight.

SEA TRAIN HOUSE

ARCHITECTURAL FIRM
Office of Mobile Design

DESIGNER
Jennifer Siegal

LOCATION
Los Angeles, California

YEAR
2003

When Richard Carlson, a Los Angeles developer who spends six months of the year traveling, decided to build a new house for himself, the last thing he had on his mind was green design. He wanted a home that would fit his recently single, semi-retired, globetrotting lifestyle. He also wanted to use up some of the materials lying around the East Los Angeles salvage yard where his family-owned construction firm stored old equipment and other random objects. "I wasn't thinking about sustainable architecture at all," he says. "It just made sense to build with what's here and to use the industrial materials I've known and worked with all my life."

←|↑ **Wedged in between a scrap metal yard and an industrial building in a gritty section of downtown L.A., the lush, tropical garden fronting the Sea Train house appears like an oasis behind the property's decidedly urban front gate.**

The result is a hidden patch of emerald rainforest in the middle of one of the most industrial neighborhoods of downtown Los Angeles—and even more surprising, one of the more ecologically sensitive houses constructed in the United States in recent years. The reason is simple: the home is almost completely recycled. Nearly all of the structural elements in the 2,600-square-foot house were already on site.

The vision for the project was partly Carlson's and partly that of his architect, Jennifer Siegal, a devotee of sustainable construction methods and of buildings on wheels who also has some rather unconventional ideas about houses—for example, she dislikes "the idea of walls." Carlson and Siegal met in the late-1990s, when Siegal was earning her degree at the Southern California Institute of Architecture and living in the Brewery loft complex, which is directly across the street from Carlson's new house. Carlson and his father had developed the lofts, turning a former Pabst Blue Ribbon building into artists' live-work studios. "They gave me a lot of free materials," says Siegal, who founded her own firm, Office of Mobile Design (OMD), to develop dynamic structures that rest lightly upon the land. "The first thing they donated was a trailer. That was the beginning of a conversation we had around recycled materials."

Carlson decided to live next to the lofts, which he manages, because he did not want to waste time on a commute. He earmarked a 50-by-200-foot strip of the facing blacktop lot for his soon-to-be built home. The site is bounded on one side by the rear wall of a light-industrial factory. He surrounded the other exposures with a 12-foot-high wall of giant steel slabs. From the street, the front gate's rusty surface looks menacing—privacy and security were important considerations—but it also evokes the austere beauty of a Richard Serra sculpture.

Nothing prepares the visitor for what lies within. The house, which is located at the rear of the property, is completely eclipsed by a lush and pungent garden that appears like an oasis behind the big steel gate. To get to the front door, one must pass around a nasturtium-covered berm, then walk along a winding path next to an 85-foot-long stream and a waterfall (which uses recycled water) and hundreds of varieties of plants that Carlson, a lover of the tropics, has imported from all over the world. The flowers and shrubs attract colorful butterflies and dragonflies year-round. Hiding in the vegetation are families of tropical turtles and firebelly toads, two iguanas, and several chameleons. Wildly varied, the garden, which was designed by James Stone, insulates the house from its jarring environment.

Carlson wanted to reuse the metal containers that had been sitting in his storage yard for years. It was partly about saving money and partly about his "love affair with industrial materials," he says. The generic, 40-foot-long by 9-foot-high seagoing containers can be purchased for $1,500 each. (The industry is moving to 53-foot-long containers, so the old ones are classified as junk.) The idea was to stack two on either end of the house, put a roof above them, and create a central living space in between.

It was Siegal's first full-scale residential project. Carlson acted as general contractor and, according

↑ The exterior fish pond, set off to one side of the garden, is made from a salvaged produce trailer.

↑ Lit up at night, the house resembles an exaggerated box lantern, glowing brightly at the end of the long garden path.

to Siegal, "he made it very, very clear from the beginning that the project would be about the client, not about the architect." This meant that he wasn't after an architectural statement, but a place that would be tailored to his needs. "I knew I wanted an uncluttered, minimalist space," he explains, but in the end, "Jennifer came up with all the shapes." She also gave the project a level of polish that belies its industrial roots as scrap metal and shipping containers.

The house, which took three months to build and sits three feet above the ground on reclaimed earth, is a simple arrangement of steel-and-glass volumes. The central living space is separated from the garden by an expansive glass wall. The slanted roof is supported by two massive, inverted steel beams. The crossbeams are made of recycled Douglas fir from a local construction site (the bedecking for the ceilings is also recycled). The roof insulation, which Carlson helped to devise, circulates cool air via narrow shafts from the shady lower section of the roof up toward the exposed higher end.

Siegal and OMD senior designer Kelly Bair sliced open, extended, and connected the shipping containers to form a unified house with a series of clearly designated functions. Each of the original trailers had its own architectural program. The master bedroom falls under the roof's highest section, connected to a sky-lit bathroom. Underneath is a media room and library. On the opposite side of the house, the top container functions as an office and lounge while the bottom one houses mechanical units, a guest bathroom, and a laundry room. Translucent sliding doors of laminated glass separate the upper-level spaces. Carlson's friend David Mocarski, principal of design firm Arkkit Forms and a professor at Art Center College of Design in Pasadena, designed all the custom cabinetry and chose the interior colors throughout the house.

The defining feature of the main living-kitchen-dining area is a waterfall by Rik Jones of Liquid Works that supplies recycled water to an indoor fountain, home to a school of ornamental koi and Chinese carp. Carlson wanted it for climate control (he prefers a humid atmosphere to the typically dry desert air of downtown Los Angeles), but it also creates a visual anchor that pulls the house together. The pool, and its counterpart in the garden on the other side of the glass facade, are made from recycled produce trailers, also from Carlson's yard. He had the wheels taken off and added layers of epoxy insulation before sinking it into the cherry-wood floor of the living room.

Carlson is a tidy man who travels a lot, so the place looks impeccably clean. The Zen simplicity of the interior forms a perfect complement to the ethic of practical yet beautiful sustainability that inspired the structure in the first place. "Everything was here already," Carlson says. "What Jennifer and I did was figure out a way to lean it all together."

ADAPTIVE RE-USE OF MATERIALS
The house's structural elements are old sea-going storage containers, some of which had been on site before the project began.

NATURAL LIGHT
With a glass curtain-wall facade and strategically placed exposures on the side and rear elevations, the house uses nothing but natural light during the day.

RECLAIMED WOOD
The massive Douglas fir crossbeams, which support the cantilevered roof, were reclaimed from a nearby construction site.

NATURAL MICROCLIMATE
The lush front garden, which includes a stream fed by recycled water, generates cool breezes and fresh air, both of which are lacking in Sea Train's asphalt-covered neighborhood.

City

←← The interior koi pond, made from an old trailer, is aligned with the exterior pool, creating the illusion of one continuous body of water.

↙↙ The front end of the master bedroom container was replaced with an arrangement of glass and steel that allows for ventilation and views of the garden.

← In the living room, a 15-foot-high flagstone waterfall that runs on recirculated water masks the stairwell leading to the master bedroom.

↙ Elevated windows, pale gray slate, and banana-colored walls enhance the natural light in the minimalist bathroom.

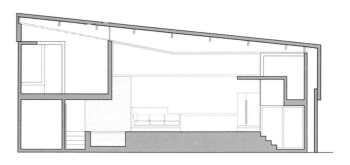

Front Section

Second Floor Plan

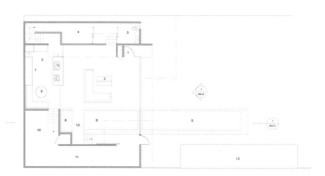

Main Floor Plan

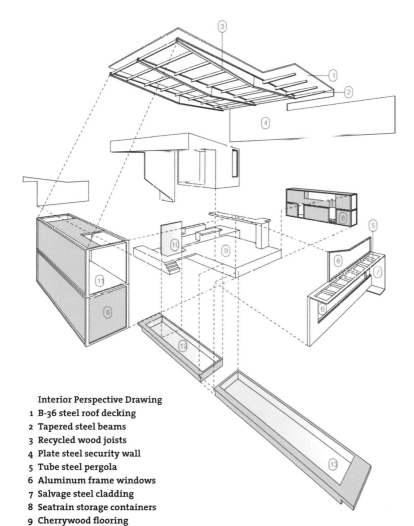

Interior Perspective Drawing
1 B-36 steel roof decking
2 Tapered steel beams
3 Recycled wood joists
4 Plate steel security wall
5 Tube steel pergola
6 Aluminum frame windows
7 Salvage steel cladding
8 Seatrain storage containers
9 Cherrywood flooring
10 Flagstone water wall
11 Recycled carpet
12 Aluminum grain trailer koi pond, interior
13 Aluminum grain trailer koi pond, exterior

THE SOLAIRE

ARCHITECTURAL FIRM
Cesar Pelli & Associates Architects

DESIGNER
Rafael Pelli

LOCATION
New York, New York

YEAR
2002

While the Manhattan skyline is full of instantly recognizable icons, the days when the Big Apple stood at the forward edge of architecture are largely in the past. The tallest skyscrapers are now rising in Asia, and the latest technical engineering innovations are more likely to be realized in Europe. Until the redevelopment at Ground Zero prompted a recent surge of public interest in architecture and urban design, bottom-line pressures and preservation struggles tended to dominate discussions about architecture in New York City.

← ↑ **Facing west across the Hudson River at the southern tip of Manhattan, the Solaire has embedded photovoltaic panels that capture sunlight throughout the day and even at dusk, above, as it bounces off the water.**

An exception to that rule is Battery Park City, one of New York's most progressive urban planning ventures in the past three decades. Built on 92 acres of landfill created by excavating the World Trade Center site in the 1960s, the mixed-use development hugging the southwestern edge of Manhattan has functioned as a laboratory for a new approach to urban living, one that combines proximity to culture and commerce with amenities available to few New Yorkers—harbor views, a marina, and finely landscaped parks embellished with public art. One of its boldest experiments was establishing, in 2000, a set of environmental guidelines requiring all new housing to be "appreciably ahead of current standards and practices for development." The Solaire, a 27-story apartment building at the southern tip of the development, is the first residential tower in New York to systematically embrace sustainable design and the first to comprehensively satisfy Battery Park City's green guidelines.

"I think of the Solaire as a great big guinea pig," enthuses project architect Rafael Pelli, a principal at Cesar Pelli & Associates. "It will educate an industry across a big sector, and education is a huge part of bringing sustainable building practices into the mainstream."

Pelli, who grew up watching his father, architect Cesar Pelli, design the master plan and several buildings for Battery Park City, and his mother,

landscape architect Diana Balmori, create parks and urban gardens, developed an early interest in sustainable design. After joining his father's New Haven, Connecticut–based practice in 1989, he opened the firm's New York City office in 2000. The Solaire commission also came in 2000, following the announcement of the new guidelines.

From the start, one of the biggest challenges for Pelli and his team was translating what they knew as general principles of sustainable building methods into specific design decisions. "There is a huge gap between the technology that exists and what is actually available from manufacturers," says Pelli. For example, the photovoltaic cells that fit the budget came only in blue, not the originally specified charcoal color. Ultimately, Pelli embraced the blue tiles; their lively, light-reflecting surfaces create a stippled quality that works well with the building's taut-skin facade. Other decisions were dictated by the team's self-imposed commitment to working with local manufacturers—half of all materials used in the construction were procured locally and another fifth had to be manufactured within 500 miles.

Pelli's team went to great lengths to make the right environmental choices at every stage. Materials and systems were tested and designs revised accordingly. A plan for bamboo flooring was scrapped when the adhesive backing was determined to be toxic. New insulation was added after an elaborate wall model—built full-scale and tested in a wind tunnel at the developer's expense—indicated that one extra layer of sealant could make a huge difference in terms of limiting air infiltration. "It turned out to be a simple solution—one guy with a goop gun goes in and the whole thing is taken care of," Pelli says. "But without those studies we would never have known it was necessary."

Incorporating a long list of sustainable technologies, the Solaire surpasses all current environmental guidelines in effect in New York. It is 35 percent more efficient than the State Energy Code requires. The tower generates 5 percent of its energy with the help of 3,400 square feet of

← Two pesticide-free terrace gardens planted with native grasses provide a private retreat for the residents and a means of natural insulation for the building.

↑ With 3,400 square feet of photovoltaic panels, among other energy conserving elements, the Solaire uses 67 percent less electricity during peak hours than comparable buildings.

↑ All the interior surface materials and paints—in both the public spaces and the individual apartments—contain no off-gassing chemicals.

photovoltaics integrated into its western facade. Most of the electricity is harvested in the summer months, when power plants struggle to keep up with the city's air-conditioning demands. Natural gas absorption chillers, high-efficiency lights and appliances, acoustic and ceramic tiles, window treatments, and interior surfaces were all selected for their energy efficiency, low toxicity, or high percentage of recycled content.

In the lobby, daylight sensors regulate artificial light levels in response to changes in natural light levels. In public stairwells and corridors, lamps are triggered by motion sensors. And inside the apartments, master switches encourage tenants to turn off all lights before walking out the door.

All of the apartments, which average 1,000 square feet, are outfitted with low-emission glass that allows sunlight to pass through while preventing heat loss as well as low-VOC paint, recycled-content carpeting, and water-sparing plumbing fixtures and toilets. A blackwater plant in the basement purifies and recycles wastewater to flush toilets, circulate in the evaporative cooling tower, and irrigate the landscaping. Rooftop plantings provide protective shade in the summer and insulation in the winter. A storm water retention tank connected to the "green roof" collects the water for later use.

The cooling, heating, and ventilation systems were designed to benefit both the environment and the tower's occupants. In fact, the building's indoor air quality is superior to the outside air. Windows open to allow in the harbor breeze while a centralized air system filters, humidifies, or dehumidifies depending on the season. Air conditioning runs on natural gas rather than electricity and uses water instead of ozone-depleting coolants. Efficiency-enhancing features include an exchanger that recovers heat from the air and uses it to create hot water.

High-tech sustainable solutions do come at a cost, especially when there are new regulations and no precedents to follow. The Solaire's construction ran about 8 percent above the costs of neighboring Battery Park buildings, which are already on the high end for New York. But for the developer, the up-front investment in efficiency pays off in tax credits and lower operating costs in the long run. The benefits to the residents' quality of life are harder to quantify, though no less significant. For the city, the Solaire's success has generated a new awareness of how sustainability can be effectively incorporated into the urban fabric—a value that speaks for itself.

Suburbs are everywhere,

everywhere cities are found. Conceived as a kind of utopia that would allow city workers to live in pastoral surroundings, the suburb, with its voracious appetite for open space and low-rise, low-density development, has turned out to be one of mankind's more harmful intrusions on the environment.

Indeed, the ballooning size of the typical new suburban home—now averaging more than 2,500 square feet in the United States—and the infinite replication of lawns, garages, septic tanks, heating systems, laundry rooms, and other amenities for each household has made the suburb a convenient metaphor for wastefulness in modern society. Even weekend homes on sites outside of traditional, planned suburbs—what wealthy New Yorkers, for example, call "the country"—are getting bigger and more extravagant. Primary residence or vacation retreat, these houses, at their most wasteful, are less about living closer to nature than an architectural ploy to have one's cake and eat it too—to combine the convenience of an urban area with the private open space of the countryside.

While architects are making great strides in bringing sustainability to the suburbs, they continue to face unique challenges there. A site for a house in the desert can be picked in accordance with sustainable planning principles—for example, on the southern incline of a hill, instead of the northern. But a typical quarter-acre suburban plot permits no such flexibility. In large tract developments, prospective homeowners usually have no say over what materials or construction methods are used or how a house is sited. Ecological solutions, however, can be introduced during subsequent renovations.

If suburbs are truly to go green, planners must look beyond the classic stand-alone family house with private garage and front and back yards. Real progress toward sustainability depends on increasing density and reducing individual house size. The embodied energy in building materials accounts for most of the energy used in construction, so smaller homes and semi-detached or townhouse-style buildings can help to reduce overall ecological impact. Such designs also reduce heating and cooling costs and allow functions such as laundry, storage, parking, and gardens to be shared with neighbors.

There is no shortage of successful models along these lines. London's Garden Suburbs of the 1910s and 1920s provided an early example of how to rethink the balance of individual and collective space in suburban developments. And from the German Siedlungen of the 1920s and 1930s to postwar Scandinavian experiments in suburban density, most notably, by Arne Jacobsen and Jørn Utzon, architects have long sought to provide models for a "compressed suburbia." More recently, the New Urbanist movement has raised valid concerns about suburban sprawl and neighborhoods that are scaled for cars rather than people.

One of the suburb's most damaging ecological consequences—pollution from residents' long daily commutes—cannot be mitigated by architecture alone. But other issues, from energy efficiency to the use of recycled materials to driveways that use permeable paving instead of asphalt, can be directly addressed by designers. And for those suburbanites and weekend-home buyers lucky enough to build from scratch, the opportunities for sustainable solutions are limited only by the imagination.

Of course, new homes are often subject to community building codes that determine size, color, setback distance, and other features. But within the confines of even the most rigid neighborhood rule book, new houses can be sited for optimal solar exposure, constructed from local, renewable materials, and equipped with maximally efficient heating, cooling, and waste systems. And when the neighbors hear how much the owners of the new sustainable house down the block are saving on their energy bills, they may just rally for a greener set of community planning regulations.

SOLAR TUBE

ARCHITECTURAL FIRM
Driendl Architects

DESIGNER
Georg Driendl

LOCATION
Vienna, Austria

YEAR
2001

The quiet residential district of Döbling, on the northwestern edge of Vienna, is not the kind of place you'd expect to find one of the most startling works of green architecture built in recent years. But nestled in a heavily wooded site in a neighborhood of high-priced single-family homes there, Georg Driendl's Solar Tube house looks like the stuff of science fiction. And in a way, it is. Unconventional aesthetically and environmentally, the house pushes the style and science of sustainable architecture to the extreme, transforming a single, energy-saving technology into a design concept for a whole building.

← Stacked three floors high on a small, wooded lot, the Solar Tube is architect Georg Driendl's idea of a twenty-first–century tree house.

A "solar tube" is a small light-and-heat capturing device that is typically installed on the roofs of high-efficiency homes. In the hands of the Vienna-based Driendl Architects, it has shaped the design of the entire house. Using the principles of radiant heating, thermal massing, and passive solar collection together with large expanses of low-emission thermal glass, the building is designed to maintain a temperature of 68 to 77 degrees Fahrenheit. Both light and heat come into the house through what Driendl calls "isolation" glass. A two-ply glazing widely used in Austria, Germany, and other middle and northern European countries (thanks to progressive legislation that mandates energy efficiency), it contains a layer of metal sandwiched between the two sheets of glass that conducts the short, warming rays, while deflecting the longer, damaging UV rays. The house's central core of reinforced concrete absorbs and stores the warmth, keeping the whole house within a comfortable temperature range.

Built in only five months, the Solar Tube exemplifies Driendl's commitment to designing for energy and cost efficiency during the construction process as well during the life of the building. His affordable building method revolves around a standardized concrete core and pre-fabricated steel skeleton pieces that are designed to "snap into place," he explains. The steel frame, which both supports the building and gives it its unique form, is kept on the inside of the glass paneling. This arrangement protects the steel structure by preventing its exposure to the climate's extreme temperature fluctuations, which can stress and weaken the steel.

Designed for two doctors and their three young children, this structure is just one iteration in a series of "Solar" houses—including Solar Deck, Solar Box, Solar Atrium, Solar Cube, Solar Blade, and Solar Trap—that Driendl has built or designed with the same energy-efficient principles. "We created the Solar series in response to research about our climate in Austria," says Driendl. "Although the coldest part of the winters only last a few months here, the region generally requires indoor heating for about half the year. All of our Solar houses require only three to four months of heating—this is the greatest source of energy saving for us Austrians and we manage to do it without high-tech equipment or high prices."

Set on a tight lot with tall trees, the 2,500-square-foot house takes maximum advantage of light and shade all year round. In the winter, defoliation exposes the house to an abundance of solar energy, which it captures through the isolation glass and stores in its massive concrete core for heat throughout the cold months. During the warmer summer months, the house is protected from overheating by thick foliage as well as a ventilation system that acts as a chimney, funneling warm air up and out. Wherever possible, Driendl used local materials—maple wood from a nearby forest, granite from a nearby quarry— and pre-fabricated parts for all the integrated furniture, including kitchen cabinets, library bookshelves, and various storage units that he designed to match the building.

Like a rounded glass "tube," the glazed walls slope strikingly around the curved, wood-covered steel structure of the three-story house. Up top, a

semi-transparent sliding roof increases ventilation and the family's proximity to nature. On the upper-level mezzanine, each of the four bedrooms enjoys two exposures. Below the sleeping quarters, the main floor allows for an open-plan arrangement of kitchen, living, and dining areas. And on the ground floor, the design accommodates a large foyer, a storage room, and an office. Thanks to textured glass

floors on the two upper levels, the house becomes its own atrium, with the tree-shaded roof visible all the way from the ground floor.

"I like to think of it as a tribute to the children," says Driendl. "For them, it's like living in a tree house. What a good way to teach them about the love of nature."

↑ The Solar Tube's rear facade, which faces north, features a downward-facing angle that diverts the high rays of the summer sun.

→ The front facade is inclined upward so that the house can absorb the warming southern light.

ISOLATION GLASS
Dual-ply windows containing a thin metallic layer that attracts winter's short rays while deflecting summer's long ones help regulate interior temperatures.

CONCRETE CORE
A massive base of reinforced concrete serves as both structural anchor and passive solar collector, absorbing heat during the day and then slowly releasing it at night.

CHIMNEY EFFECT
In the warm months of summer, the retractable glass roof provides a convenient escape hatch for rising hot air as well an easy ingress for cool breezes.

LOCAL MATERIALS
Driendl used locally quarried granite as floor covering for both the first and second levels and maple wood grown in a neighboring forest for the custom cabinetry and furniture.

← On the ground floor, the entire rear facade opens garage-door–style onto the garden, eliminating the division between indoors and out.

↑ With a glass ceiling, the house's third story, which contains all four bedrooms, funnels light down to the two levels below.

↑ An open staircase and inlaid glass floor panels on the second story keep the kitchen and living rooms, as well as the ground-floor offices below, flooded with natural light.

→ The cool angularity of the prefabricated interior steel support structure is offset by curved, wood-covered beams that define the Solar Tube's unique form.

→→ Even the bathrooms are enclosed by the same wide swaths of glass used in the more public areas of the house. Strategically placed opaque panels ensure privacy.

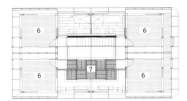

Second Floor Plan
6 Bedroom
7 Gallery

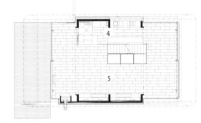

Ground Floor Plan
4 Kitchen
5 Living room

Basement Plan
1 Foyer
2 Office
3 Technical room

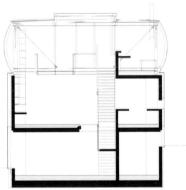

South Section

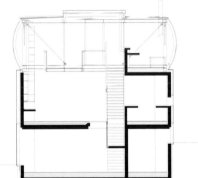

North Section

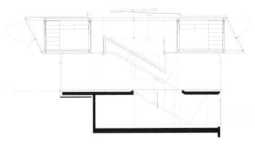

West Section

CHARLOTTE RESIDENCE

LOCATION
Charlotte, North Carolina

ARCHITECTURAL FIRM
William McDonough + Partners

DESIGNER
Allison Ewing and William McDonough

YEAR
2002

Charlotte, North Carolina, a banking center and one of the fastest growing cities in the southern United States over the last couple of decades, has a population of more than half a million. But you'd never know it from looking at the five-acre piece of land for which the Charlottesville, Virginia firm William McDonough + Partners — long a leader of the green-design movement — designed this two-story, three-bedroom house. Though the house sits within the Charlotte city limits, its rustic exterior finishes and sprawling, leafy grounds make it seem much further removed from urban life than the twenty miles that separate it from the heart of downtown.

← The site for this McDonough + Partners design sits within the Charlotte city limits but has the look of a secluded retreat with its canopy of loblolly pines, which the architects worked hard to protect.

"The site is essentially a hundred-year-old forest," says Allison Ewing, the McDonough + Partners architect who led the design team. The property is dominated by stands of loblolly, or yellow southern pine trees, which grow thin and tall — up to 100 feet, in some cases. On this site, they've woven their branches together over time to form canopies that provide shade and an always-shifting variety of light patterns.

"We asked the client when they hired us to get a survey done," Ewing adds. "Not just the site contours but a real tree survey. That identified the key, really beautiful trees we wanted to design around."

Positioning the house along axes already defined by the existing trees was the firm's first step in defining sustainability on this particular project. "Bill talks all the time about how and when we become indigenous to place, native to place, ourselves," Ewing says, referring to William McDonough, the firm's founder. In addition to running his thirty-person firm, McDonough is a noted author and frequent lecturer on sustainability and a partner in the design and consulting firm MBDC, which advises companies, including multinational corporations such as Ford,

about how to design and produce without waste, or according to the principals of what he has termed "cradle to cradle" design.

For the Charlotte house, it wasn't just a matter of knocking down as few trees as possible during the construction process. The architects aimed, from the outset, to create interior spaces that would mimic the experience of standing outdoors on the site. They also designed a vaulted roof above the main living areas to suggest the expansive sense of a canopy rising above.

"When you get right down to it, we think people deep down would rather spend their days outdoors," Ewing says. "So we try to create architecture that gives them that feeling."

Other features of the design pointed toward the same experiential goal. The ground floor is generally open and fluid in plan, with high cabinets helping to divide the space and broad expanses of low-emission windows for abundant light. Two fieldstone walls, perpendicular in plan, run through the center of the L-shaped house.

"Originally the client came to us saying they wanted a stone house," Ewing says, "but a house entirely of stone was going to be prohibitively expensive. We felt we could give them the sense of having a stone house by combining wood and glass with the prominent stone walls." The walls within also help ground the house in a firm horizontality, drawing the eye back outside, in what Ewing calls "a key element in integrating the house with the landscape." Also important in reaching that goal was the firm's work with the landscape designers on the project, Nelson Byrd Woltz.

The result of that constant emphasis on marrying house and site is what Ewing calls "both an anomaly in its urban setting and an archetype: a home in the woods."

And since this is a McDonough + Partners house, the green elements don't end there. A geothermal system, which taps into the heat of the earth by digging several hundred feet down into the ground, provides radiant heat. (Because of high installation costs and because few residential builders have

↑ Since the North Carolina
climate allows residents to spend
time outdoors nearly year-round,
the house is designed to provide
easy exterior access.

→ The facade's stone base is
echoed in the gravel landscaping
by Nelson Byrd Woltz Landscape
Architects.

↑ The interior spaces sit under a vaulted roof that the architects designed to resemble a canopy of tree branches. High cabinets and freestanding walls divide the house into discrete rooms while maintaining the sense of a loft-like open space.

experience working with them, geothermal systems remain a rarity in single-family homes, even those that aspire to high levels of green design.) All the wood used in the house is either reclaimed, like the eastern white cedar siding, or certified as sustainably harvested. The trees, not surprisingly, offer good shading in the summer, aided by deep roof overhangs. In winter there is good heat retention from passive solar orientation, though Ewing says that "we weren't dogmatic about orienting the house directly to the south. It was a synchronicity between passive solar and the views." In addition, no formaldehyde or vinyl was

used, and all the materials are non-toxic and were bought locally where possible. The walls are made of SIPS panels, a super-efficient building material that sandwiches a polystyrene core between two layers of oriented strand board, or OSB.

Still, every architect at McDonough + Partners would tell you that green design fails the minute it becomes a mere checklist. "We try to define sustainability as broadly and holistically as possible," Ewing says. "You can figure out a million green features, but in the end it's about the clients, how they live, and their health and well-being."

↑ The view of the surrounding
woods is accentuated by large,
gridded windows. Sunlight floods
the interior during the winter,
when the sun is low enough to slip
beneath the exterior overhangs.

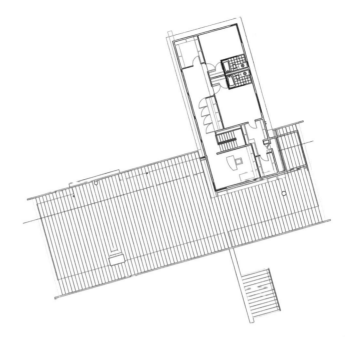

Second Floor Plan

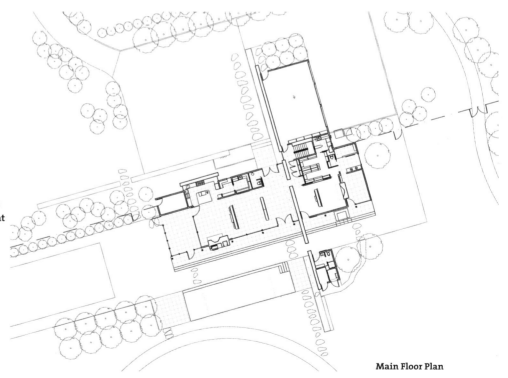

→ The inverted L-shaped plan is
bisected by a fieldstone wall that
runs through the interior and
extends outside.

Main Floor Plan

VILLA SARI

ARCHITECTURAL FIRM
ARRAK Arkkitehdit

DESIGNER
Hannu Kiiskilä

LOCATION
Pori, Finland

YEAR
2000

Though the winters in Pori, a town on the west coast of Finland about 120 miles northwest of Helsinki, aren't as frigid as those farther north in the country, the region is nonetheless a place of extremes. In the dead of winter, the sun stays above the horizon for a few precious hours, hanging low in the sky. In the summer, it sets only briefly. The spread between a year's lowest and highest temperatures can top 100 degrees. Because conditions can be harsh and winter heating bills high, says architect Hannu Kiiskilä, "we have good reason here to pay attention to sustainability."

← ARRAK's Villa Sari is located on a rocky site near the western coast of Finland. Its horizontal design soaks in winter sun and uses deep overhangs to provide shade to outdoor spaces in summer.

Kiiskilä's design for a young couple and their three children keeps those considerations at the forefront while also producing a remarkably assured piece of architecture. The Villa Sari is a four-bedroom, 2,500-square-foot home mostly on one level, with a finished basement below and generous exterior space—a rarity for this region—that allows for a mixture of indoor and outdoor activities in nice weather. The structure acts as both a barrier against winter cold and as a breathable shell. The exterior materials are hardy—they include rectangular panels of a stiff laminate made of recycled newspaper and coated in resin—but they also promote a visual sense of variety and openness.

"We have a tradition in Finland of making very warm boxes," says Kiiskilä, a principal in the Helsinki firm ARRAK Arkkitehdit, "with barriers between outside and inside that are very strict. Our houses don't give us very many opportunities to extend our living spaces to the outdoors. Here, we've tried to use a very flexible arrangement, which keeps the house warm in an efficient way in winter but also open to the land, to the sun, and to the air."

The site, a rocky outcropping about five miles inland from the Gulf of Bothnia, which separates Finland from Sweden, offered some natural advantages in that regard. Sloping down gently from north to south, it allowed Kiiskilä to expose the southern edge of the house, which holds the dining area, kitchen, and a courtyard, while tucking three bedrooms on the northern side into the rocky hillside. (A fourth bedroom is below, in the basement.) The courtyard is thus usable through much of the year, warmed by southern exposure and protected by a U-shaped extension of the wings of the house—with the kitchen on one side and a sauna on the other—around it. A second outdoor terrace, constructed of stone quarried at the site, extends from the western side of the house.

Solar loss and gain are tightly controlled in a number of ways, beginning with the building's orientation. The windows on the southern facade are relatively large, but they are covered with moveable louvered panels aligned to block summer sunlight while letting winter sun stream into the house. A thin band of clerestory windows along the top of the facade is similarly positioned to maximize winter sunlight indoors. In addition, the windows have a reflective glazing on the inner layer that bounces heat back into the interior before it can escape.

With the exception of some Canadian cedar in the latticework, all of the wood used in construction—mostly pine and fir—was grown within a few dozen miles of the site. The air circulation system is even more ambitious in terms of sustainability. It constantly moves approximately 60 percent of the interior air through the house, filtering it and mixing it with air from the outside as it does so; this helps keep the temperature inside the house steady from one end to the other.

It also helps keep the heating bill low. When the fireplace is lit, Kiiskilä explains, the heat is distributed throughout the house. All in all, the architect estimates that the Villa Sari uses about three-quarters as much energy as a typical house of its size in this part of Finland.

In plan, the house is organized around a central

open kitchen. The rest of the rooms spin out from there in a sort of flywheel pattern, with a dining area and adjacent sunken living room in one direction and the sleeping quarters in the other. South of the bedrooms is a sauna—practically a requirement in any Finnish home.

From the outside, the house suggests a cubist assemblage of interlocking boxes arranged along a horizontal plane—as if one of Frank Lloyd Wright's prairie-style houses had been crossed with the work of a Scandinavian modernist.

↑ The southern facade is covered with hard laminate panels made of recycled newspaper and coated in resin. Windows are shaded by adjustable louvers.

← The site's existing pine and fir trees, which were carefully protected during construction, enclose the house on its western edge.

↑ Nestled into the undulating terrain, the house is outfitted with large windows that permit unusually good exposure on its southern side.

South Elevation

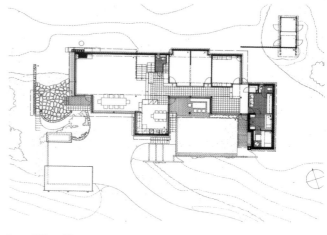

Second Floor Plan

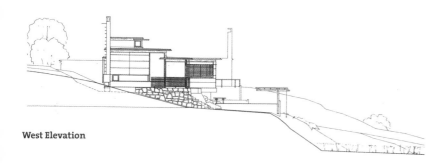

West Elevation

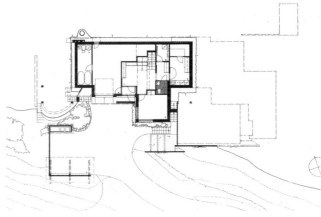

First Floor Plan

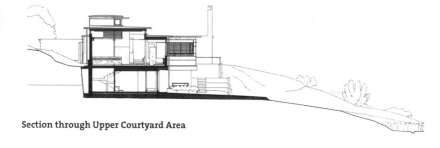

Section through Upper Courtyard Area

Section through Living Room Area

←↑ An ambitious circulation scheme allows heat from the fireplace to flow throughout the interior. The windows' interior reflective coating keeps heat from escaping during the winter.

LITTLE TESSERACT

LOCATION
Rhinebeck, New York

ARCHITECTURAL FIRM
Steven Holl Architects

DESIGNER
Steven Holl

YEAR
2004

Steven Holl is one of the best-regarded American architects of his generation, well known for designs including the Kiasma Museum in Helsinki and Simmons Hall at M.I.T. He was also a member, with architecture-world heavyweights Peter Eisenman, Charles Gwathmey, and Richard Meier, in the so-called Dream Team group that was named a finalist in the master plan competition for the World Trade Center site. What he hasn't been known for is a commitment to sustainable architecture.

That may change, however, once more architects, critics, and environmentalists get a look at the Little Tesseract, an addition to Holl's own weekend house in Rhinebeck, New York, about 80 miles north of Manhattan. The new structure—which was largely finished by 2004, though Holl says he is still tinkering with it—adds about 1,200 square feet of space on two levels to a small existing stone house built in the 1950s. By any standard the addition qualifies as green. And it is also perhaps less of an anomaly for Holl than it would appear. He says he has been exploring a range of sustainable strategies in recent projects, including a geothermal project in Nanjing, China.

The first sustainable decision Holl made in Rhinebeck was not to tear down his existing house, which was built of fieldstone gathered from the property itself. "The original house is small," he says, "but I figured, why tear something down if it's good? Why not just expand it?"

That was a little bit easier said than done, as it turned out. The existing house is U-shaped, and although it would have made the most sense to extend the new, light-filled wing toward the south, to take advantage of winter sunlight, that edge of the old structure forms the closed-off end of the U, which made an addition there impractical. So Holl came up with a plan to build the new structure on the opposite side, at the open end of the U. The addition takes the form of an L-shaped structure in steel and glass wrapping around two sides of a new, slightly warped cube. Sheathed in stucco painted a charcoal-gray color, the cube is punched through with steel-framed windows. The L-shaped portion of the addition, on the western and southern sides of the new cube, forms what Holl calls "a temperate zone," helping retain warmth from the sun in winter and bring in cooling breezes in summer.

At the same time that he was beginning to sketch plans for the addition, Holl was working on a new architecture school for Cornell University (a project that ultimately fell through). The concept at Cornell was to build the new architecture school using the tesseract, which is essentially a four-dimensional version of a cube, as a symbolic guidepost, suggesting an effort to expand the traditional architectural cube. ("What a square is to a cube," Holl explains, "a cube is to a tesseract.") That project, with a budget of $25 million, was taking up most of his creative attention; not surprisingly, ideas from Cornell began to overflow into his work on the weekend house—enough that Holl began referring to it as the Little Tesseract.

At Cornell, Holl wanted to include a huge stack of glass planks on the south and east walls that would take advantage of the so-called chimney effect. In the winter they would absorb sunlight and slowly release it back into the building. In summer they would draw warm air up and then release it at the top of the building. Holl had received some sample versions of the glass planks from a manufacturer, and he decided to put them to use in Rhinebeck. "I put them in as an experiment," he says, "but it's been an experiment that has really worked. On a sunny day when it's 30 degrees outside the studio upstairs is close to 70 degrees, without turning on the heat."

In warm weather, the planks combine with other features to keep the house cool. Breezes come along a specially designed pond, which is fed exclusively by rainwater collected from scuppers on the roof. Then those breezes are drawn up the solar stack wall, which has summer vents open at the top.

← Steven Holl's addition to his own weekend house north of New York City is positioned near a pond. A smaller pond was also added immediately adjacent to the house to help cool approaching breezes.

← The two-story addition is made up of a warped cube covered with charcoal-gray stucco and punched through with steel-frame windows.

↑ The so-called temperate zone in the addition created a new dining room lined by large, hinged windows that pivot out almost completely to promote natural ventilation.

↗ The addition includes a studio above a bedroom and dining room, with a small triangular patio. Glass planks line the southwest facade.

As Holl explains, "All the windows in the steel L are hinged, and they pivot out to open almost completely so that it can become essentially an outdoor space in summertime. The wind blows right through. We don't have air conditioning, and you know what? We haven't missed it. On a really hot day, if the house has been shut up, you open those windows and pop the skylight, and you can drop the temperature 20 degrees in about 15 minutes."

Holl's final green touch on the building, literally, will be planting a sedum roof on the addition to help keep it cool in summer. The roof of the original house already signals Holl's interest in

sustainability: it is covered with photovoltaic solar panels that the architect added in the late 1990s.

"When we had that huge blackout [in the summer of 2003]," Holl recalls, "we happened to be up at the house. Everybody else was going out to buy gas generators and then had to line up at the gas station." While his neighbors fiddled with their generators, Holl was able to relax inside thanks to the power generated by the solar panels. "It's not a huge amount if that's all you're relying on," he says, "just enough to power a few light bulbs, a stereo, and a fan for one room. But for those nights that was the perfect amount."

Site Plan

→ | →→ The addition is designed to maximize light and air. The new dining room is surrounded by windows.

↘ | ↘↘ A stair leads from the dining room to the studio above. A ladder leads to the roof.

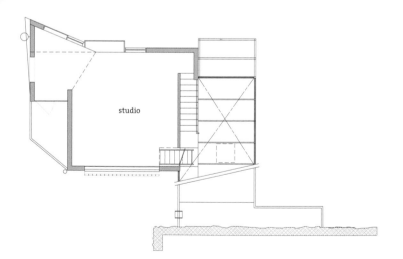

studio

Second Floor Plan

bedroom

cooling pond

dining room

First Floor Plan

→ The public rooms of Arkin Tilt's compact Breeze House are contained in a single double-height space with large clerestory windows. A load-bearing storage wall divides that space from bedrooms on the other side.

← An exterior fireplace makes socializing outdoors possible despite Northern California's cool summer evenings.

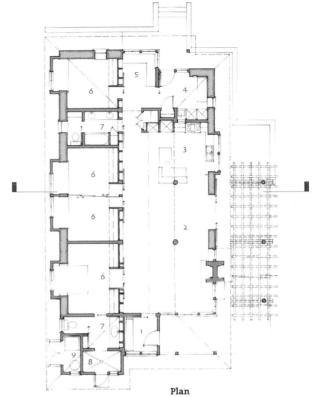

← Openings in the long interior storage wall give way to bedrooms; these two are separated by a sliding door that can be opened to connect them.

Plan
1 Entry
2 Living/dining room
3 Kitchen
4 Laundry
5 Office
6 Bedroom
7 Bath
8 Shower
9 Mechanical room

← The kitchen includes columns of unfinished, locally harvested eucalyptus; countertops that contain recycled glass; and a hatch that allows the residents to put recyclable material into a bin that can be accessed directly from the outside.

Section

NAKED HOUSE

ARCHITECTURAL FIRM
Shigeru Ban Architects

DESIGNER
Shigeru Ban

LOCATION
Kawagoe, Japan

YEAR
2001

In the late 1990s, an unusual fax came chugging through the machine at Shigeru Ban's Tokyo office. A man who wanted Ban to design a new house for his family—and whom Ban had met just once before—was writing to make some very precise and unusual requests about the project. The note explained that the man, who was in his thirties and lived with his wife, his two children, and his seventy-five-year-old mother, wanted a house for all of them that, as Ban remembers the man describing it, "provides the least privacy, so that the family members are not secluded from one another—a house that gives everyone the freedom to have individual activities in a shared atmosphere, in the middle of a unified family."

← Shigeru Ban's Naked House, designed for a three-generation family, is made up of a completely open two-story building envelope within which four portable bedrooms, raised on casters, can be moved around. Curtains help turn the open kitchen, for example, into a private space.

Even in Japan, a country known for tight family bonds and for residential architecture that takes pains to respect them, this was a startling design goal: as *little* privacy as possible. It was certainly enough to pique the interest of Ban, who, as one of the most talked-about young architects in the world, and one of the busiest, receives far more requests for design help than he can possibly accommodate. (It also helped that the man transmitted his thoughts in the form that he did: the peripatetic Ban, who keeps his office small and rejects the usual trappings that accompany his level of prominence, is known for communicating almost exclusively by fax.)

"It always takes some time of careful thinking before accepting a private residential project," Ban explains. "I often wonder if what I want to achieve as a designer, in a project, meets the client's needs and desires for his home, without either of us having to compromise our own beliefs."

This project suggested none of that compromise. The client himself, after all, was the one who wanted to pursue a radical design, asking Ban in effect to re-imagine the way family space is divided within a house. The budget also presented a challenge—

and for Ban, a challenge is almost always a positive thing—because the family wanted to spend only 250 million yen, or about $225,000. And so Ban accepted the commission and got to work on what turned out to be a highly unusual house about 1,700 square feet in size. The architect calls it the Naked House because of how exposed and unadorned he has left its structure and rooms.

The site is near a river in Kawagoe, a city 30 miles or so north of Tokyo. Though Kawagoe has a population of more than 300,000, the site for the Naked House is quiet, even pastoral. Ban himself describes the agricultural setting as located "by a river and...surrounded by fields, with greenhouses here and there."

It is from those greenhouses, more than any modernist precedent, that the spare, supremely functional Naked House takes its aesthetic cues (though certainly the way it does so recalls the way early modern architects looked to grain elevators and warehouses instead of churches and villas for their formal inspiration). The design is basic: a double-height rectangular shell, made of corrugated plastic panels affixed to a wooden frame and lined on the interior with sheets of nylon attached with Velcro strips. Insulation is provided by clear plastic bags—the same type used to ship fruit—stuffed with polyethylene foam. During the day, the interior is lit by soft, diffuse light filtering through those materials.

Along the edges of the main rectangular space are a few fixed elements, like a kitchen (which can be closed off by drawing a curtain), and a bathroom. In the middle of the structure float four open, rolling boxes, raised on casters and open on two sides, which serve as bedrooms. In profile these mobile units recall the boxes that magicians pull together and apart while they seemingly saw a woman in half. The bedrooms can be joined together, their sliding doors removed, to create a larger combined space; but individually they are small, Ban says, in order to encourage simplicity and minimal furnishings, and to allow them to be moved around more easily—even, in good

↑ The simple exterior form, with its minimal number of doors and windows, is meant to evoke the greenhouses rising from the fields nearby.

weather, to the outside. Essentially Japanese tatami rooms on wheels, they combine with the basic building shell to create the ultimate open plan.

What makes the house green, exactly? More than anything, its modest efficiency of materials, size, and budget. The amount of materials Ban used was stunningly small given the fact that he was being asked to create a custom house for a family of five. The design is full of elements that can be reconfigured or simply used for more than one function. The tops of the rolling bedrooms, for example, serve as play areas for the children. And Ban has clearly thought inventively about ways of

lowering the operating costs and use of resources. The architect suggests, for example, rolling the bedrooms near the air conditioning units on warm days or the heaters on cold ones, to keep the family comfortable while keeping energy demand down.

Perhaps it is the house's nakedness, both literal and figurative, that makes it most green: it is completely comfortable baring the ways it solves its architectural and budgetary challenges. It is a radical design, but it is also hospitable and full of lessons for any architect or client who wants to live simply and stylishly at the same time.

↑ Set into basic wood stud frames, the wall panels are made of corrugated plastic on the exterior and lined with nylon fabric on the inside. Clear plastic bags stuffed with polyethylene foam inserted in between serve as insulation.

← A covered breezeway is lined with a series of doors instead of windows that can be opened to bring in light and air.

↙↙ The portable bedrooms-on-wheels can be joined together to create larger, combined spaces. Weather permitting, they can even be moved outside.

↙ The bathroom, like the rest of the house, is designed as a series of contiguous spaces that can be enclosed or kept completely open.

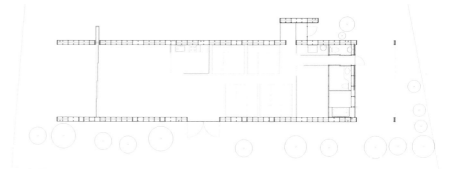

Floor Plan

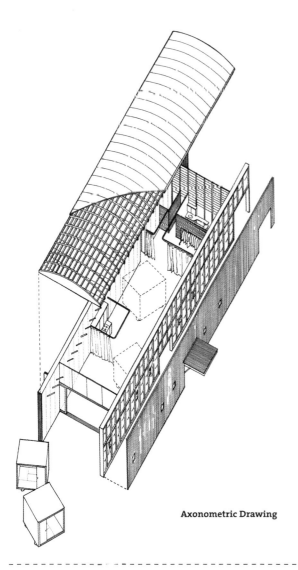

Axonometric Drawing

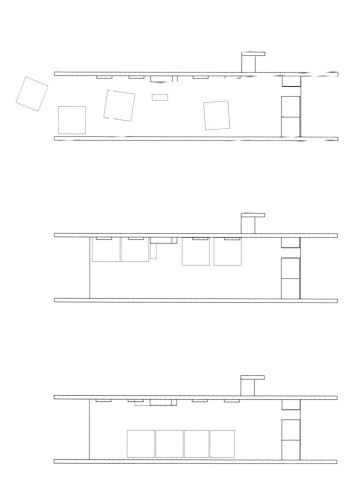

Alternate Configurations of Rolling Bedrooms

More than ten billion acres

of the Earth's surface are covered in forest, and most of that land falls in sparsely populated mountainous regions. These stunning landscapes, among the last to resist industrialization, urbanization, and suburban sprawl, are essential to the survival of the planet. They promote water and soil conservation, provide flood control, synthesize huge amounts of oxygen, help protect against climate change, and promote long-term biodiversity.

But more than 140,000 acres of forested land are being destroyed every day. Although great strides are being made in forest management and conservation, just 2 percent of forests worldwide are officially protected, the majority of these in Europe and the United States. And while most of the problems that plague mountainous regions won't be solved by architecture alone, it's not hard to see that building in these areas carries its own specific responsibilities.

The mountainside's often-steep, elevated terrain also suggests its own specific architectural gestures and responses. In no other geographic landscape does residential design take its cues so directly from the landscape. Historically, mountainside houses have displayed an aesthetic of rough-hewn durability and timelessness. And while contemporary examples are a far cry from the log cabins and mountain lodges of the popular imagination, they share with those earlier buildings a taste for the vernacular and a loyalty to local materials. Part of that has simply to do with remoteness: it makes little sense, practically or environmentally, to haul exotic materials halfway up a mountain and, as a result, the architects who work in such regions have learned to use local stones and even boulders—natural building blocks found close by. And assuming the forests from which it comes are managed sustainability, wood can be an eco-friendly building material.

Mountainous building sites, like those in the tropics and desert, face the challenge of extreme weather. Houses must withstand freezing temperatures and frequent rain and snow, and protect themselves against the possibility of mudslides. The sun, when it shines, can be harsher at high altitudes than at sea level. But these extremes also make it possible for green architects to take advantage of solar and wind power, and even the rushing water of rivers and streams, to generate electricity. Snow accumulation and frequent rainfall permit the harvesting of fresh water.

Architects working in the mountains have to be particularly mindful of the landscape. During construction, it makes sense to limit the use of heavy trucks and machinery, and to minimize the damage to existing trees and plants, whose shade-giving properties and protection against erosion will be missed if they are knocked down while the house is going up. Finally, it's worth remembering that a house on a mountain slope is more visible than one on a flat piece of land, which means its architecture will necessarily have a visual impact on more than just its immediate neighbors. This doesn't mean that contemporary design is automatically inappropriate in such areas, or that architects ought to rely exclusively on traditional or quiet facades when building houses on the mountainside. It simply means that sightlines from the outside in have to be considered as carefully as those from the inside out.

HOUSE WITH SHADES

ARCHITECTURAL FIRM
Achenbach Architekten + Designer

DESIGNERS
Joachim and Gabriele Achenbach

LOCATION
Jebenhausen, Germany

YEAR
2000

In the Bavarian section of the Tessin, a scenic stretch of lake-laced Alpine foothills at the intersection of Italy, Switzerland, and Germany, tradition governs home-building in both style and structure. Wood frames, thick walls, vaulted ceilings, and white-trimmed windows are part of the regional protocol. But when a local couple approached Achenbach Architekten + Designer — a high-tech firm known for bravura steel-and-glass structures — to build their new home, they knew they would not end up in a quaint villa with geranium-filled window boxes.

The clients, a German doctor and her British husband, a stay-at-home dad, were "open to unconventional building solutions," says architect Joachim Achenbach, who has overseen the small eponymous firm in Stuttgart with his wife and partner, Gabriele, since 1990. Unconventional is exactly what they got. In look and in function, the sharply rectangular energy-efficient house is unlike anything the small village of Jebenhausen and its 1,500 residents have ever seen. With an exposed steel frame, floor-to-ceiling windows, and a prominent exterior awning system, it looks more like a chic urban storefront than a rural chalet. The interior is similarly anomalous. Its open, light-filled space has nothing in common with the layouts of neighboring homes, which adhere to the traditional practice of dividing living areas into clusters of cozy rooms.

Despite appearances, site-specificity guided the Achenbachs' every design decision. From its sub-grade entryway to its rooftop pergola, the house has the high-altitude aptitude of a championship skier. The three-story structure is nestled deep into a narrow, sloping plot; its transverse placement on the site allows for a southwest orientation. An insulated-glass curtain wall optimizes the solar benefits of the region's bountiful sunlight while affording panoramic views of the snow-capped Schwäbische Alb, the region's towering peak,

ten miles away. The house's most prominent feature, a row of retractable textile shades that runs the entire length of the facade, makes a bold defense against unwanted solar gain in the searing summer months without blocking out the magnificent mountain vistas.

Composed of a series of intersecting boxes, the house has four bedrooms, three bathrooms, an open living-dining area off the kitchen, a garage, and a finished basement resting on a reinforced-concrete base. The residential portion, which measures 25 feet deep by 43 feet wide, sits within an exterior steel skeleton, which extends almost 60 feet lengthwise. A central staircase ascends from the sunken ground floor to the top-level garden, connecting all the private areas to the open, double-height gallery that runs the entire length of the middle floor. Interior sliding doors made of translucent light-diffusing glass provide a measure of privacy in the otherwise open interior.

For their teenage daughter, the clients requested the addition of a spacious music room and workshop, which the Achenbachs placed in the partially submerged ground level, next to the canopied main entrance. The front door had to be located on the valley side due to ingress constraints on the site, a drawback that the architects turned to the house's advantage: sinking the entry on one side of a thin trench sliced from the garden not only makes room for an external staircase, which smoothly connects the garden and veranda, it also allows light to penetrate the sub-grade rooms.

Energy efficiency is the thread that binds the various elements of the house together. The Achenbachs' goal was to introduce as much natural light into the interior as possible, allowing the space to capture and store solar heat and reduce artificial lighting needs during the day. The high ratio of insulated envelope surface to building volume maximizes these effects. A mechanically controlled ventilation system (with a thermal mass exchange unit) works in concert with the exterior shading to minimize heat loss and regulate temperatures. Two large solar panels on

← Joachim and Gabriele Achenbach's sensor-driven automatic shades block the sun but not the Alpine views.

← In the winter, the exterior shades stay up nearly all the time, allowing the warming rays of the sun to help heat the house.

↙ In the summer, the shades are raised or lowered depending on sun and weather conditions. A solar sensor triggers automatic adjustments based on light levels.

→ Laminated wood floors, ceiling panels, and siding made from locally grown pine trees help to visually and acoustically soften the glass-enclosed spaces.

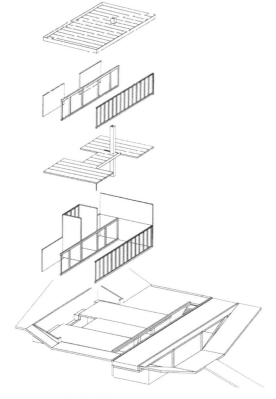

Axonometric Drawing

the roof transform sunlight into electric power for heating water, while a series of photovoltaic cells generate enough energy to fuel the air-circulation system. A wood-burning stove, which depends on air circulation for heat distribution, generates extra warmth in the cooler months. When even more heat is needed, a gas-burning heater does the trick. Native grasses planted on the roof absorb the abundant rainwater, improving the house's microclimate and mitigating excessive runoff, the main source of the frequent flooding that plagues the area.

The house's textile shading system extends over the entire southwest facade and terrace. When drawn down, the nylon panels, which hang off a steel truss a few feet out from the glass front, extend the spatial boundaries of the house. Strategically deployed light and wind sensors automatically regulate the optimal amount of sun and heat exposure, triggering the shades to rise or descend accordingly. In the summer, the nylon shades are programmed to follow the sun and to fold up in periods of heavy wind. In the winter they stay up nearly all the time.

The Achenbachs, whose practice ranges from new construction to preservation work to experimental structural innovations (for example, they developed a high-load-bearing laminated glass tube that functions as a building block), have experimented with shade systems before, but never on this scale. "We were very glad to find clients who were willing to try it, and even more glad that they ended up liking it. They love the fact that when the shades are drawn, the interior still seems very large."

Tucked in among its traditional neighbors, the house makes no pretense at trying to fit in. Still, it was only after the planning process, when the house was actually built, that the clients began to realize just how much it would stand out. These days, the project has become something of a destination, especially for architects and design buffs, who frequently come by to see it. "The clients needed a couple years until they were strong enough to cope with the difference," Joachim Achenbach says. "Now they feel fine. But as far as I know, the neighbors still think the house is strange."

SOLARHAUS III

ARCHITECTURAL FIRM
Schwarz Architektur

DESIGNER
Dietrich Schwarz

LOCATION
Ebnat-Kappel, Switzerland

YEAR
2000

When it comes to Dietrich Schwarz's SolarHaus III, the Roman numeral tells a story. The house, which sits in a low-rise, low-density collection of single-family designs in the Swiss town of Ebnat-Kappel, looks simple. Its long wood and glass profile is attractively spare and rectilinear, and noticeably horizontal against the rising backdrop of the Alps. But the building's very simplicity also represents a substantial breakthrough for the architect when it comes to his approach to green design.

‹ **This low-lying and supremely efficient wood and glass design by Dietrich Schwarz is set against an idyllic landscape he knows well — the Alps — in the small Swiss town of Ebnat-Kappel.**

↑ **The main entrance is tucked away near the rear of the house, at the end of a gravel path, and thus doesn't interfere with the spare regularity of the wide southern facade.**

Schwarz's first SolarHaus was finished in 1996 in the nearby town of Domat/Ems. It now holds the architect's offices as well as a rental apartment for a young family. In that design, completed when Schwarz was just thirty-two years old, the architect used a host of cutting-edge, even experimental, green features. It was the first building, in fact, in which Schwarz employed Power Glass, a material of the architect's own invention that is attached to a structure's facade. It absorbs solar energy with an unusual level of efficiency while also allowing some translucency to help light the interior. SolarHaus II, meanwhile, was finished in 1999 in Gelterkinden, near Basel. It is a bold, modernist building that looks a bit like a cube raised on stilts. If it appears perhaps a bit less futuristic than its predecessor, it nonetheless stands out on its site as a visitor from some other place.

SolarHaus III is different. It is the simplest of the three projects but also a savvy, effective combination of new materials and age-old knowledge about making the most of a site. Its design suggests an architect who is comfortable enough with his talent to step back from bold gestures and concentrate on efficient, well-made architecture — not unlike a writer whose style grows sparer and less flashy as he becomes more confident and experienced.

"The first SolarHaus was like a Formula One race car," Schwarz says. "It had a very high budget, because we were trying out a lot of advanced techniques. It was a manifesto, in a way, to draw attention to the progress we were making with solar materials. But the house in Ebnat-Kappel is different: it's actually more efficient than the first one and at the same time was built for very little money."

Indeed, the house is something of a case study in modest efficiency, featuring the kind of sustainability that doesn't call any attention to itself. The single-story, two-bedroom, one-bath house measures only about 900 square feet. On the north, east, and west sides, it turns a timbered facade with very few windows to the outside world. Those paneled surfaces are filled with energy-efficient cellulose insulation made mostly from newspapers.

The southern facade, in contrast, is made up entirely of alternating bands of triple-insulated glass and Power Glass. The roof of the house slopes up from north to south, allowing the southern facade to catch as much winter sun as possible. For Schwarz, the profile created by the slope suggests what he calls "a revival" of the Modernist credo "form follows function" in the service of environmentalism.

In his first two solar houses, Schwarz says he was preoccupied with pursuing "a gain strategy": that is, using Power Glass and other materials to create as much electricity from the sun as possible. But in doing so, he admits, he lost sight of the "loss strategy": keeping a tight lid on the amount of energy lost in the cold Swiss winters. In Ebnat-Kappel, he tried combining the two approaches, and the result is a zero-energy house—an airtight box that produces 100 percent of the electricity it needs for its operation. For Schwarz, the third time really has been the charm.

← The roof of the house slopes up, allowing the southern facade to be as tall as possible. Glass panels alternate with bands of Power Glass, a material Schwarz invented, to catch and store the winter sun.

← The Power Glass panels appear greenish-blue when seen from the inside.

→ The simple interior features
unfinished plywood panels on
the walls, ceilings, and floor.

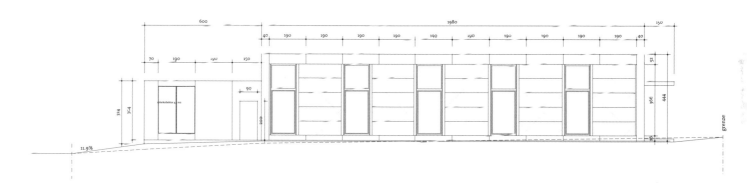

South Elevation

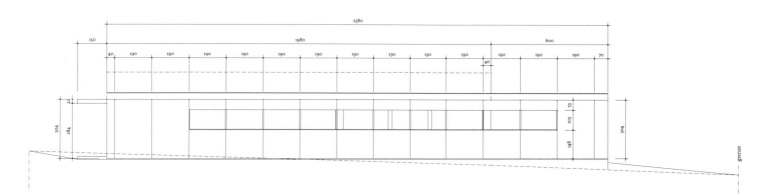

North Elevation

GREAT (BAMBOO) WALL

LOCATION
Commune by the Great Wall, Shuiguan-Badaling, China

ARCHITECTURAL FIRM
Kengo Kuma & Associates

DESIGNER
Kengo Kuma

YEAR
2002

Fifty-one-year-old Kengo Kuma, among the best-known Japanese architects of his generation, tends to use each of his residential commissions to explore a single building material. In a dense Tokyo neighborhood, for example, he designed the so-called Plastic House, in which nearly all the walls and floors (and even the screws) are made of a translucent, luminous plastic the color of green tea. Finished in 2002, it is a surprisingly beautiful piece of architecture — a meditation on the hidden aesthetic properties of a material rescued from the scrap heap of the design world.

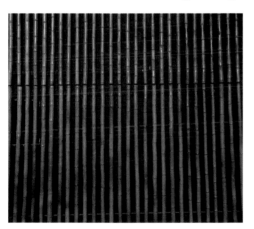

← Kengo Kuma's bamboo house north of Beijing includes an open-air tea house, which seems to float above a shallow reflecting pool. The space provides views of the surrounding hillside, on top of which the Great Wall itself stands.

↑ Of bamboo, the architect says he finds "charm in the material's weakness."

In his design for a villa in a new development north of Beijing called the Commune by the Great Wall, Kuma used the same approach — and displayed the same knack for wringing beautiful forms from commonplace materials — in building a house that is as much an ode to bamboo as a house constructed from it. Bamboo is one of the most sustainable materials architects and builders have at their disposal, because it grows so quickly that its stocks can be replenished very efficiently. Commonly mistaken for a type of tree, bamboo is actually a grass, which helps explain the rate — among some varieties, several feet per day — at which it shoots upward.

The Commune by the Great Wall, planned by the ambitious Chinese husband-and-wife developers Pan Shiyi and Zhang Xin, features eleven private villas and a clubhouse, each designed by a leading Asian architect. Along with Kuma, the list includes Shigeru Ban from Japan, Gary Chang and Rocco Yim from Hong Kong, and several mainland Chinese architects. The development is located in the shadow of the Great Wall, about an hour's drive north of Beijing and only six miles from Badaling, the spot where most Western tourists visit the wall.

The developers hope to eventually sell the houses (or copies of them on a secondary site up the hill) to private owners. But at least in the first phase

of the development's existence, as a marketing vehicle, the villas are being rented out on a per-night basis to tourists and for corporate gatherings, forming the most exclusive — and probably among the most expensive — boutique hotel in Asia. The Great (Bamboo) Wall house, for example, rents for $1,088 per night — a fee that includes the services of a private butler.

Kuma's design for the house borrows its low horizonal profile from the Great Wall itself. But while the Wall symbolizes permanence, solidity, and exclusion, Kuma's bamboo wall is meant to suggest the easy transfer of light and breezes from one side of the house to the other, as well as a certain lightweight, unfinished, and even fragile quality. Of bamboo, Kuma says he finds "charm in the material's weakness."

The heart of the plan is a delicate tea house that floats on a square pool just outside the living room and is surrounded by what Kuma calls a "scaffold" of bamboo that offers privacy as well as views of a mountainside that is dense and green even in winter.

The house is also designed to mimic the way the Great Wall, as Kuma puts it, "runs almost endlessly along the undulating ridge line without being isolated from the surrounding environment." Kuma wanted to keep the house long and low rather than have it stand out as an object, with a single story at grade above a basement level. That shape helps the house look smaller than it is.

The design probably doesn't qualify as the most modest project in Kuma's portfolio. Indeed, the Commune development has already drawn fire from critics who take issue with the way it cheekily uses icons of Chinese communism (beginning, of course, with the word "commune" itself, and continuing with the Maoist uniforms — all black with a red star pin — worn by the staff) as branding and marketing tools as it tries to sell luxury housing to the country's growing ranks of entrepreneurs.

Those criticisms notwithstanding, Kuma has done much here to dramatize the design possibilities of bamboo, just as he did with plastic in the Tokyo

↑ The house, with its long, horizontal profile, is designed to mimic the Great Wall, which runs along the ridgeline above.

↗ Both inside and on exterior walkways, Kuma plays up the contrast between the polished marble flooring and the rough bamboo siding.

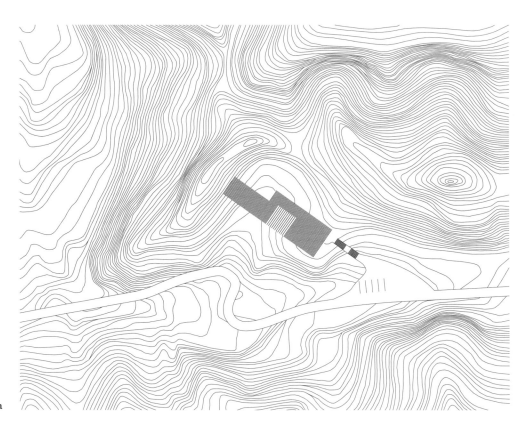

Site Plan

↑ Both the kitchen and the dining room have a bamboo-clad ceiling.

house. Who knew, after all, that bamboo could be sculptural, or cast such a variety of shadows, or add rhythm to a facade so effectively? If Kuma thus inspires other architects to trade mahogany or some other endangered hardwood for this most friendly of environmental materials—especially in China, where there is rising demand for American-style residential excess and no green design movement to speak of—his decision to accept the developers'

invitation to take part in this early stab at Chinese luxury housing will be fully justified.

Kuma has also shown how luxurious sustain-ability can appear if put in the right architectural hands. In the end, the house may wind up operating as a kind of architectural Trojan horse, helping to sneak green-design ideas behind the lines drawn by zealous developers.

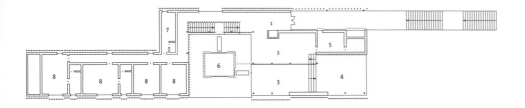

Main Floor Plan

1 Entry
2 Kitchen
3 Dining room
4 Living room
5 Storage
6 Lounge
7 Bathroom
8 Guest room
9 Machine room
10 Staff room

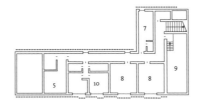

Ground Floor Plan

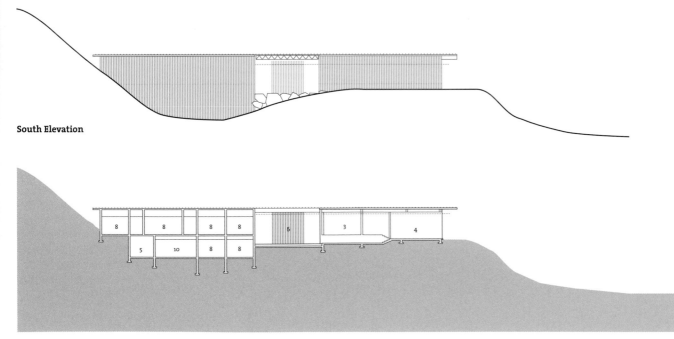

South Elevation

Section

↑ The tall windows of the living room provide expansive views of the lush hillside nearby.

R128

ARCHITECTURAL FIRM
Werner Sobek Ingenieure

DESIGNER
Werner Sobek

LOCATION
Stuttgart, Germany

YEAR
2002

Werner Sobek's design philosophy is simple. "Architecture is environmental design. It therefore mirrors society, its behavior and ambitions," he says. The four-story residence Sobek designed for his family in 2002 is an elegant embodiment of that credo. The glass house is so efficient, it actually generates more energy than it uses. Its open-plan interiors and its high-tech features—touch-screen temperature controls, computer-controlled heating system, voice-activated doors, and radar-controlled faucets—say a lot about social behavior in a technologically advanced society. Its sleek, impeccable design projects an aesthetic ambition rarely seen in sustainable buildings. But Sobek did not set out to create a high-tech wonder: "I was governed by the ideal of living in three-dimensional transparency so that I could always feel close to nature. The technology just helped me achieve that ideal."

← Facing southwest on a steep hillside outside Stuttgart, Werner Sobek's R128 is an emmission-free house that requires no external energy input for heating or cooling.

Sobek, who has a doctorate in structural engineering and is director of the Institute for Lightweight Structures and Conceptual Design at the University of Stuttgart, spent a year at Skidmore, Owings & Merrill in Chicago in 1982 on the first Fazlur Khan fellowship, which has been awarded twice since. His architecture remains firmly rooted in the ideals of modernism, and his firm, Werner Sobek Ingenieure, which has 110 people working in Stuttgart and three others in New York, has consulted on such large-scale projects as the Bangkok International Airport and the Sony Center in Berlin. His futuristic R128—so named after its street address, number 128 Römerstrasse—is a compendium of Sobek's ideas and research about sustainability, energy conservation, and recycling. With its allusions to Mies van der Rohe's Farnsworth House and Philip Johnson's Glass House, it is clearly intended as the latest chapter in the history of transparent case study houses designed by modernist architects.

Perched on a steep hillside overlooking downtown Stuttgart, the crystal box of a house has a glass-skinned steel frame that was erected on site in a mere four days. The building reuses the cement foundation of the dilapidated 1923 house that once stood there. Designed to be installed and dismantled with minmal impact on the land, the modular structure arrived in just one truckload. Every part can be easily detached and recycled. The wooden floors, for example, are made of prefabricated panels that are suspended between the steel I-beams without screws or bolts. All pipes and communication lines are concealed in shallow troughs behind removable laminated metal covers positioned along the floors. Since the house contains no plaster walls, almost nothing would have to go to waste if the structure were ever demolished.

The steel framework that holds the house together weighs only 10 tons. It consists of twelve pillars reinforced with a network of horizontal and diagonal I-beams. Additional cantilevered steel elements and external staircases and walkways complete the house. Visitors enter through a steel footbridge on the fourth floor, which contains the living and dining areas. Bedrooms for Sobek and his wife and for their son as well as additional living, office, and service areas are located on the lower floors. All floors are completely open and flexible, with the exception of a two-story unit that houses the toilets and bathrooms.

The house brings together some of the most up-to-date energy management technologies available to home builders today. "My goal was to build a house that would be perfectly green, more ecologically advanced than anything to date: that was the challenge I set for myself," says Sobek. "I didn't want to create something that future generations would have to cope with, so I made sure everything is easily recyclable." The coated and triple-glazed 90 by-53-inch window

panels—which have the insulating properties of 4 inches of rockwool and had never been used in residential construction before, according to Sobek—allow solar radiation to pass through the facade and into the house, where it is absorbed by water-cooled panels in the ceiling. A heat transformer conveys energy to an accumulator, which then releases it over the colder months through ceiling radiators. The triple glazing also makes sure the house doesn't overheat in the summer (there are no shades or curtains inside the home; privacy is provided by trees). Electricity is generated by forty-eight roof-mounted photovoltaic cells. In peak times the house draws energy from the public network, but on balance it actually adds energy to the municipal power grid. Because it is completely self-sustaining, the house produces no emissions of any kind.

Life in this radical glass box may not be for everybody. Convention clearly takes a back seat to purist design solutions, like the absence of door handles, switches, and closets. The architect and his family own only a few items of furniture, several pieces designed by Sobek himself. There is not much privacy or creature comfort in a house so directly exposed to nature. However, for enthusiasts of architectural minimalism and high-tech sustainable solutions, R128 has few peers. It is a functioning laboratory for the home life of the future.

↖ All of the electrical energy needed to power the house is supplied by forty-eight frameless solar panels embedded in the roof. The system uses the public grid as a zero-loss energy store, tapping in only when there's an energy shortfall.

← The triple-glazed panels of the facade contain a metal-coated plastic foil that deflects the long infrared rays that would pass through normal glass and overheat the space.

SOLAR PANELS
The electrical energy needed to run the mechanical ventilation system is supplied by solar receptors embedded in the roof.

SPLIT-SYSTEM AIR CONDITIONING
Each floor has a separate temperature control, which allows the system to cool or heat only the space being used.

RECYCLABLE MATERIALS
From the wood panel flooring and glass walls to the bolted steel skeleton, every component of the house was chosen for its capacity to be recycled.

TRIPLE GLAZING
With three layers of glass containing a film of metal-coated plastic foil in the air space between the outer and central panes, as well as inert gas between each layer, the windows have an extremely low heat transmission value.

NATURAL LIGHT
Floor-to-ceiling windows eliminate the need for artificial light during the day.

Mountainside

The floors consist of prefabricated, plastic-covered wood panels that are less than 2.5 inches thick and rest on beams without screws or bolts.

Aluminium panels clipped to ceilings incorporate an accoustically absorbent surface as well as the lighting system and water-filled pipe coils for heating.

Energy studies for summer daytime, summer nightime, and winter show the changes in both incoming and outbound air temperatures.

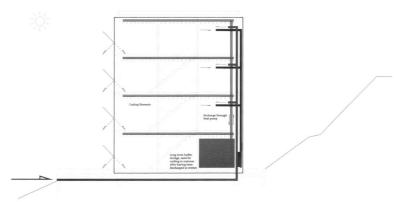

Energy | summer daytime

The four-story staircase and large openings in the floorplates create a feeling of continuous vertical space. The absence of internal partitions extends the space horizontally.

Bathrooms are the only enclosed spaces in the house. Opening and closing their opaque doors requires swiping a hand in front of an infrared sensor.

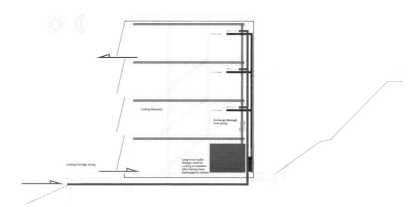

Energy | summer nighttime

All pipes and cables for electricity, water, and communication systems are run in aluminium ducts along the inside of the facade.

The exposed internal duct system allows for maximum flexibilty. A free-standing bathtub, for example, may be "plugged in" to the water line at any point simply by opening the appropriate duct.

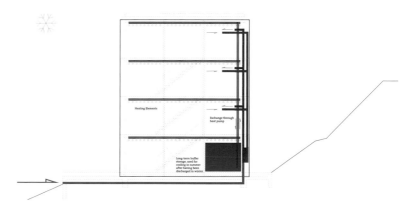

Energy | winter

While few of us make a living from

the sea or a river these days, more and more people are moving to the water's edge. Communities small and large are dismantling ports, repurposing docks, and greening embankments for the benefit of their citizens and businesses. The recent evolution of cities like Barcelona, London, and New York has been closely tied to the renaissance of their once-decrepit waterfronts, with the rehabilitation or addition of residential units there among the most prominent improvements.

Throughout history, however, most waterfront homes have been built as places of escape from the city. From secluded cabins to modern beach houses to lakefront retreats, such homes are usually designed to maximize a sense of connection to nature and even to the elements; for this reason waterside living has long been synonymous with sensitivity to the natural environment's beauty—and its vulnerability.

It is no coincidence that some of the most notable experiments in rethinking the principles of residential development and community life have occurred in waterside locations, both because they are seen as isolated, even utopian sites and because they can be so fragile. Here as elsewhere, green design goes hand in hand with progressive approaches to land use and urban planning. Amsterdam's Eastern Harbour Docklands development, with its eight thousand row houses standing on reclaimed docks, and the paradigmatic New Urbanist town of Seaside, Florida, are good examples.

Among the most architecturally celebrated planned waterside communities is Nothern California's Sea Ranch. For over three decades, it has stood on the Pacific Coast as a touchstone for designers seeking a better balance between the needs of individual families and those of the natural environment. Early on, houses at Sea Ranch were built in clusters to enhance energy efficiency. The Condominium

One development was built of weathered wood by the firm of Moore Lyndon Turnbull Whitaker and designed to "capture the sun and shield the wind." In what amounted to a radical idea at the time, large portions of the windy bluffs were left free of development so that views of the sea and the coastal meadows could be shared by the entire community. Such macro-planning choices are just as green as the decision to add solar panels to one's roof.

Whether they are designed for relaxation or year-round living, waterfront properties are commonly exposed to extreme heat, wind, sunshine, salt, water damage, and sudden climate change. On small islands or remote lakes, waterside homes can lack access to gas, electricity, waste disposal, and even potable water. Green houses in these locations combine the necessary responses to such site conditions with technologies that maximize energy efficiency and minimize the house's impact on its surroundings. And green builders know that preserving the land on which the house sits is the key factor in protecting the water itself.

Waterside homes can exploit the advantages of their location by making use of solar or wind power, by siphoning breezes that blow across the top of a pond or lake and using them for natural ventilation, and by employing locally available, often inexpensive building materials, from beach pebbles to bamboo husks. At the same time, waterside homes have a special responsibility to preserve the natural resources of both the land and the water. Protection goes both ways—safeguarding the house from nature, and nature from the house.

The greatest damage to waterside locations stems from large-scale collective development rather than the choices made by an individual homeowner or architect. Still, overcrowding and seaside destruction happen one house at a time, and there is plenty each architect can do both to conserve the landscape and to set a standard for others to follow.

Fears about the demise of the seashore as a result of encroaching urban development have been with us for generations, and they are not likely to fade anytime soon. "We shall have before long to change our ideas about the seaside. It is losing its old glamour through being brought so near to the town," complained Ella Carter in her 1937 book *Seaside Houses and Bungalows*. With current advances in green design, our ideas about the waterside are changing once again.

HOWARD HOUSE

LOCATION
West Pennant, Nova Scotia, Canada

ARCHITECTURAL FIRM
Brian MacKay-Lyons Architects

DESIGNER
Brian MacKay-Lyons

YEAR
1999

In the small, craggy fishing villages along Nova Scotia's remote southeastern coast, local fishermen have been recycling for years. Transforming old cargo containers into boatsheds, they've created a landscape of weathered metal boxes that plainly reflects both the ruggedness and modesty of their tradition. On the edge of one such village, wedged in among the boulders of a hook-shaped peninsula that reaches into the sea, stands Brian MacKay-Lyons's Howard House.

Long and lean and clad in corrugated metal, the 110-by-12-foot, three-bedroom, single-family residence is so well camouflaged that for several years the local governing council actually thought it was just another container-cum-boatshed and taxed it accordingly. For MacKay-Lyons, a Nova Scotia native who has based his practice on what he calls "an architecture rooted in place," that miscalculation was proof of the design's success. "I think of the building as being a kind of didactic instrument that's meant to explain the cultural landscape, to enhance the sense of the place. I think of it as cultural sustainability," he says.

The Howards are an academic couple—he's an art historian, she's a librarian, and both are passionate about architecture—who decided to relocate from British Columbia to Nova Scotia with their two small children. For them, MacKay-Lyons was an obvious choice. His site-specific architectural investigations appealed to their interest in the conceptual connections between art and architecture. In early discussions, client and architect began formulating the project in terms of land art—a concept that for both parties has as much to do with artistic expression as it does with respect for the land.

Sited on a north-south axis at the western edge of a 4-acre parcel, the house incorporates a host of low-impact strategies—including passive solar collection, passive venting, thermal massing, and in-floor radiant heating—that make it not only appear to fit into the landscape but ensure its welcome

there. In addition, MacKay-Lyons chose materials that were locally available and forms that respond to the site's complex microclimate. The lack of overhangs, for example, reflects the area's constantly fluctuating temperatures. "With a regular if unpredictable freeze-thaw cycle, thanks to the warm gulf-stream air that runs through here, overhangs create leaks," he explains. "The frequent freezing and then expanding and then thawing action will wreak havoc on materials and joints."

For each of its three ocean exposures, MacKay-Lyons devised different structural and fenestration strategies. The lengthy west side, which parallels the open ocean, is defended against the prevailing winds with a concrete casement. Jutting squarely out of the house's narrow profile, it functions like a jetty or "shoulder against the wind," as MacKay-Lyons describes it. Underneath, sturdy steel trusses help the rest of the house manage the wind load. On the east side, which overlooks a glaciated landscape of shallow rocky pools, a wide swath of corrugated Galvalume is punctuated by an assortment of windows, each sized differently to frame a particular view. Facing south, where the peninsula forms a quiet bay and a beach that has become the children's playground, MacKay-Lyons placed double-height steel-frame windows for maximum solar gain. A set of sliding glass doors opens to a narrow balcony extending the house out toward the water, which is a mere 3 feet away.

The wood-frame building's monolithic pitched roof climbs to the south, toward the water. Below, one continuous, unobstructed living space progresses from garage (separated from the house by a covered breezeway and two massive barn-style rolling doors), to entry court, to kitchen and living room, and then out to the cantilevered deck. On the ground floor, three bedrooms are lined up along a corridor. Upstairs, a mezzanine loft provides a secluded space for the master bedroom and a study. "Part of the idea was taking a thin tube and domesticating it," MacKay-Lyons explains.

The other part was finding an economical means of building. With a budget of less than $200,000

← The western, ocean-facing facade of Brian McKay-Lyon's Howard House is protected against Nova Scotia's prevailing winds with a concrete casement. The southern end features a balcony that cantilevers out toward the water.

Canadian, each decision had to be about efficiency both in terms of materials and labor costs. MacKay-Lyons chose locally grown maple for the cabinetry, exposed polished concrete for the floors (even in the bedrooms, since the whole house has radiant heating), and de-laminated chip rock for the walls. The exposed ceiling reveals the structure's conventional light-timber platform framing. For MacKay-Lyons, the lack of expensive finishes and elaborate detailing did not detract from the design at all. In his view, the restrictive palette enabled

him to create a house much more in keeping with the Nova Scotia ethos. "In this place people shun ostentation. You would never want to call attention to yourself. Buildings are supposed to be frugal."

With what the architect describes as "zero detailing," the house has a clean, modern, minimal look. But this is not a heavy-handed or over-wrought minimalism: "I like to draw a line between minimalism and plainness. Minimalism is a fancy term. Plainness is the term common folks use," he maintains.

MacKay-Lyons is keenly attuned to the use of language, both verbal and architectural. For him, making reference to the vernacular is about more than clever quotations. Using the materials and forms of local buildings is his way of staying in tune with the uniqueness of his native land and helping his buildings do the same. "The only source of real sustainable building is the vernacular," he says. "The vernacular is what you build when you can't afford to get it wrong environmentally."

← The narrow, boxy silhouette of the Howard House was designed to resemble the local boat sheds Nova Scotia fishermen have been building in the area for decades.

↖ ↑ The southern end of the house is open to the water on three sides. A set of metal-framed glass doors leads out to the balcony.

←← The breezeway is clad in unfinished plywood and paved with gravel.

← The mezzanine office space has de-laminicated chip rock walls and cabinets made of locally grown maple.

↙↙ The living room features pigment-free concrete floors and maple cabinets.

↙ The staircase is made of inexpensive annodized aluminum treds.

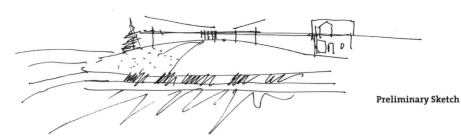

Preliminary Sketch

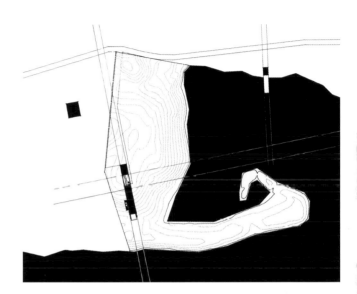

Site Plan

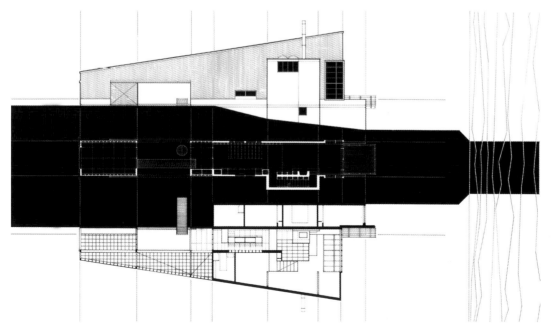

Combined Elevation, Plan, and Section

SWART RESIDENCE

LOCATION
Melbourne, Australia

ARCHITECTURAL FIRM
Cocks Carmichael

DESIGNER
Peter Carmichael

YEAR
2004

For years, Melbourne resident Ricci Swart monitored the real-estate listings for properties on Beaconsfield Parade. The two-mile stretch of stately old townhouses facing Port Phillip Bay held the promise of satisfying her childhood dream of living by the water. By the time her own kids had grown up, Swart, a multimedia producer, was ready for a change. So when she saw a for-sale sign on the very block she had coveted, she made her move. The fact that the property was a complete eyesore—the old Edwardian had been brutalized by an insensitive renovation decades earlier—only increased her enthusiasm, since it meant she could start from scratch.

← Facing Melbourne's Port Philip Bay and a busy motorway, the Swart Residence is designed to accentuate views of the water while minimizing traffic noise and pollution on the interior.

↑ Photovoltaic cells and solar hot water panels on the roof capture enough energy to make the house self-sufficient much of the year. An inverter ensures that excess electrical energy can be returned to the electrical supply authority.

Swart knew she wanted to build a sustainable house, but the 30-foot-wide lot, hemmed in on both sides by frilly, nineteenth-century terrace houses and subject to tight local building codes, presented a host of design constraints. Peter Carmichael, a principal of the Melbourne-based architectural firm Cocks Carmichael, has been experimenting with sustainable technologies in his neo-modernist projects since the 1970s. But he is also well versed in the complexities of building in historic districts. After seeing his bold yet respectful renovation of a nearby Victorian, Swart gave him the commission. Her brief was tri-fold: she wanted a contemporary house that nevertheless respected its traditional neighbors, a configuration of rooms that didn't waste any space, and materials and systems that required little or no maintenance.

The three-story concrete-and-glass residence is a house at the beach, not a beach house. With a spare, lofty aesthetic and two separate apartments—a sky-lit upper duplex with two bedrooms and a study for Swart, plus a two-bedroom ground-floor apartment that can be rented or lent to guests—it belongs as much to the city as to the seaside.

Carmichael used both passive and active solar strategies and materials that were either locally available, renewably harvested, or durable enough to withstand the effects of evaporating salt water and exhaust spewed by the passing traffic. He also paid particular attention to context. "We picked up the rhythm of the adjacent row; for example, the columns are at the same spacing as those of the houses on either side, and the arch form that sits next to the big front door is a direct reference to the neo-Italianate neighbors," he says. The freestanding frontispiece has several practical functions: in addition to framing the bay, it absorbs vibrations from the passing traffic, buffers the interior from exterior noise and gusty winds, and blocks out the burning rays of the late afternoon summer sun. Its gentle curve is angled to align the house with its two neighbors, each of which has a different setback.

Carmichael also drew inspiration from the characteristics of the site. The combination of beach, boardwalk, and oceanside motorway skirting a row of gracious homes reminded him of the Mediterranean towns along the French Riviera where Henri Matisse had painted. And the graceful, curving motifs found in *The Dance* and other Matisse works are echoed in the geometry of the Swart house, making surprise appearances throughout the interior.

The proximity of beach and motorway guided most of the design decisions, from the addition of sealed front windows that fend off traffic noise and pollution to the glazed interior airshaft that slices through the center of the house, ventilating all three levels with fresh air drawn in from a height that limits the intake of vehicular exhaust. Carmichael's aim was to optimize air quality and views of the bay while minimizing energy use. Consequently, the roof is heavily insulated and the front wall is inset with half-inch–thick glass, primarily for acoustic reasons but also because its thermal transfer resistance is much better than that of thinner glass. To the rear, overhangs control the intense north sun, permitting penetration in winter but blocking the harsh rays of summer. Photovoltaic panels on the roof are connected to the electricity grid. When sunshine is abundant, they accumulate a surplus, which is credited back to the home for use in the gray winter months.

←←|←|↙
The north-facing rear terrace, which is protected by a deep overhang and stainless-steel louvres, extends the third-floor living space, offering sweeping views of the city beyond.

→ Made of poured concrete, the semi-detached, curving facade acts as a vibration sink as well as a sun visor to shade the living room from all but the low afternoon sun.

Insulation and heat management are partly reliant on the site's preexisting characteristics—sharing side walls with the neighboring houses helps moderate temperatures—and partly through the deployment of high-tech devices. The house is wired to accommodate a fully integrated control network that enables lights, blinds, air-conditioning, security, and even landscape features to be programmed to respond to light conditions, temperature variations, occupancy circumstances, and security needs.

Rainwater collected from the roofs of both the main house and the detached garage is distributed to the back garden by an automated irrigation system. The front waterfall—a poetic form of noise reduction—runs on a separate system of recycled water. (On the advice of a hydraulics consultant, a planned gray-water system was ruled out due to the compact site area available and the likelihood of saturating and souring the soil.) Watering needs, however, are relatively minimal: rather than an incessantly thirsty lawn, Carmichael laid out a stone patio flanked by two small flowerbeds and a vegetable patch. The scheme appealed to Swart both environmentally and practically. "One of my primary requirements was that the house be easy to run, easy to take care of," she says. "I wanted to be able to walk out of the house, get on a plane, and stay away for three months without worrying about upkeep."

Other low-maintenance and energy-efficient solutions include low-voltage halogens with dimmer controls and high-efficiency fluorescent bulbs that reduce power demands. Solar hot water panels, which operate on a closed-circuit thermo-siphon system with gas boosters, offer the most efficient format for Melbourne's temperate climate, according to Carmichael. And seven separate split-system air-conditioners allow for focused heating and cooling in designated areas of the house.

"Despite all the high-tech features, or perhaps as a result of them, I've become much more connected to the environment since living here," says Swart. "Since the house is constantly adjusting itself, it makes me conscious of subtle changes in the wind and the tides and the light. And I really like that. I really like the connection."

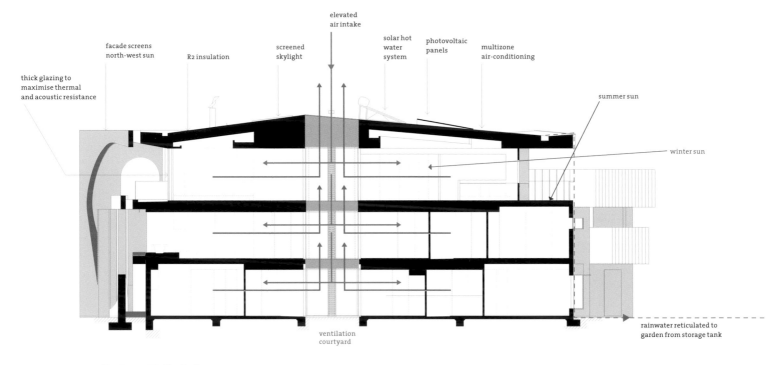

thick glazing to maximise thermal and acoustic resistance

facade screens north-west sun

R2 insulation

screened skylight

elevated air intake

solar hot water system

photovoltaic panels

multizone air-conditioning

summer sun

winter sun

ventilation courtyard

rainwater reticulated to garden from storage tank

Passive and Active Systems

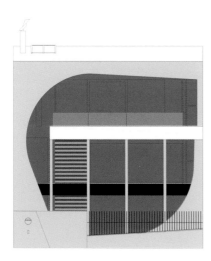

South Elevation

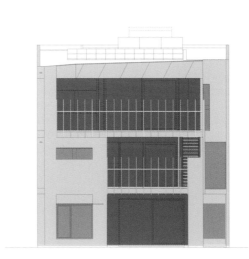

North Elevation

CENTRAL AIRSHAFT
Cutting through all three
levels at the center of the
house, the airshaft is a site-
specific feature that improves
the internal air quality by
drawing fresh air from the
exterior above the traffic line.

PHOTOVOLTAIC CELLS
The solar collectors on the
roof, which supply most of
the house's electric power, are
connected to the power grid
with a 0.2KV inverter so that
excess electrical energy can
be returned to the electrical
supply authority.

RAINWATER COLLECTION
Rain is collected from the
roofs of the main house and
the garage and distributed to
the garden by an automated
irrigation system.

AUTOMATED CLIMATE
CONTROLS
An integrated system
controls lights, blinds, air-
conditioning, and security,
and can be programmed
to respond to light and
temperature conditions
as well as patterns of
occupancy.

LAKE WASHINGTON HOUSE

LOCATION
Mercer Island, Washington

ARCHITECTURAL FIRM
Olson Sundberg Kundig Allen Architects

DESIGNER
Jim Olson

YEAR
2004

"The main idea was to make beauty out of green techniques," says Jim Olson of the house he designed at the edge of Lake Washington on Mercer Island, a predominantly suburban community just east of Seattle. Olson, a principal in the Seattle firm Olson Sundberg Kundig Allen, is known for combining the clean lines of modernist design with a Pacific Northwest regionalism featuring wood, steel, and glass.

Though he has certainly designed his share of expansive single-family residences, Olson has also shown a continuing interest in modest design and environmental consciousness. His own family cabin in western Washington, for example, which he has slowly updated over the years, is a tiny exercise in architectural restraint and sits lightly on its thickly wooded site.

This Lake Washington house, finished in 2004, is bigger but in its own way no less concerned with sustainability. Olson arranged the design around a large curved wall, sheathed in recyclable Rheinzink panels, which is 50 feet long and 28 feet tall at its highest point. The centerpiece of the house's natural ventilation system, the wall acts as a chimney to funnel air up, down, or sideways, depending on the season, and follows a U-shaped path as it curves through the center of the residence. It is aligned to follow the path of the sun atop the house's lakefront site. In summer, it pulls lake breezes through the house at its lower level and pushes warmer air out the top. In cooler parts of the year, it bounces daylight back into the living and dining rooms. The skylight adjoining it heats air during the winter; that air is trapped by the chimney and then vented down to heat the rooms.

There are other sustainable features in the design, to be sure. Radiant heating warms the floors. Part of the roof is planted with sedum, a drought-tolerant plant that helps keep heat inside in winter and repel it in summer. The handsome siding is reclaimed redwood. Trickle vents bring in fresh air year-round,

and sun-control shades not only help define the clean, contemporary look of the lakefront facade but stop the sun's heat before it enters the house. Even in the summer, no air conditioning is required.

Outside, the noted landscape architect Kathryn Gustafson, who is based in Seattle and Paris, has continued the green theme. She designed a driveway with permeable paving and added shade trees to aid climate control for the house. She retained existing trees wherever possible and added mostly native, drought-tolerant plants, along with what she calls "limited, consolidated 'injections' of ornamental plantings requiring more water."

But for Olson, the curved wall, or chimney, stands as an icon for the entire project. "The chimney becomes a sculptural form expressing its function—turning function into art," he says. It forms the backdrop for a permanent installation by glass artist Ed Carpenter, which will refract sunlight entering the house and then project it into the interior of the curving wall. Olson calls the result a "light painting."

On a symbolic level, the wall represents a successful effort to marry organic and modernist forms. The rest of the house is largely rectilinear, heavy on horizontal lines and rooms arranged as a series of boxy, redwood-covered forms. But in the end, those right angles are forced—perhaps persuaded is a better word—to yield to the curve and tilt of the wall, and by extension to the natural world.

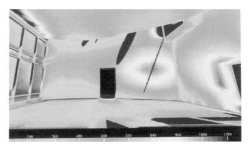

↑ The architects used a digital climate-modeling program to predict and control the effect of solar gain inside the house.

← Covered by Rheinzink panels, the house's large curved wall looks purely sculptural but is in fact hightly practical; its rounded form catches breezes coming off the lake and directs them into the house, keeping the interior cool.

← The house is a collection of boxy, modernist rooms. The sedum on the roof helps repel heat in summer and retain it in winter.

← The largely glazed lakefront facade provides the double-height living room and bedrooms with lake views. Aluminum sun shades on the windows deflect sunlight in summer.

→ | →→ Interior spaces gain drama from high ceilings. Views of the lake from the living room, and of trees from the library, are precisely framed.

→ Diagrams by Jim Olson illustrate the way the house is designed to direct breezes through the interior in summer, pushing warm air out the top of a natural chimney created by a u-shaped wall. In winter, the wall directs sunlight inside, lessening the need for artificial light—not an insignificant detail in the rainy Pacific Northwest.

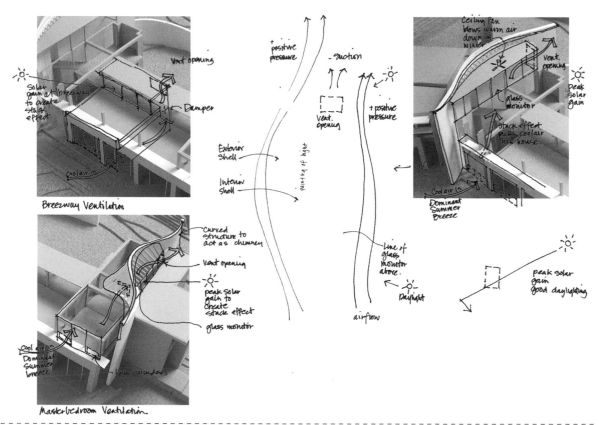

WALLA WOMBA GUEST HOUSE

ARCHITECTURAL FIRM
1+2 Architecture

DESIGNERS
Cath Hall, Mike Verdouw, Fred Ward

LOCATION
Bruny Island, Tasmania, Australia

YEAR
2003

Reaching this vacation house on Bruny (one of the smaller of several islands that make up the Australian state of Tasmania) from Hobart, the state's capital, requires the following: first, drive about thirty minutes from Hobart to the coastal town of Kettering; then take the car ferry across the D'Entrecasteaux Channel to Bruny; finally, drive about one hour, much of it on unpaved road, to a remote part of the thin island that overlooks the water in three directions, including a dramatic vista through eucalyptus and slender casuarina trees back to the Tasmanian mainland.

← This weekend house by the Tasmanian firm 1+2 Architecture uses a raised steel frame to sit lightly on its thickly wooded site, which is dotted with eucalyptus and casuarina trees and overlooks the water in three directions. Lifting the house also helps keep natural drainage patterns intact.

It was in this remote setting that the Tasmanian firm 1+2 Architecture set out to create what Cath Hall, one of the firm's three principals, calls "a hidden retreat" and "an escape from the pressures of contemporary urban living." From the start, Hall says, the firm wanted the house "to slip quietly and with minimum impact into its delicate context."

To that end, practically every feature of its architecture has been selected with restraint—and with sustainability—in mind. To begin with, the architects (and a tight budget) convinced the clients to build a house much smaller than the one they originally envisioned (the total square footage is 2,150) and to keep it to a single story. The house sits on a raised steel frame that minimized the need for excavation and keeps natural drainage patterns intact. All waste is dealt with on site, and rainwater is collected for drinking and household use. The house is completely independent of local power, water, and sewer connections. Electricity is generated by photovoltaic panels on the roof, with backup provided by a gas generator.

Overall demand for power is kept low through a number of passive-solar strategies, including high-value insulation, double glazing, and siting of most sleeping areas on the cooler side of the lot. (In the southern hemisphere, that side faces south.) On the north side of the house, the large windows take full advantage of the low-hanging winter sun. Indeed, the striking form of the house flows naturally from this passive-solar strategy: its two swooping roofs, one much taller than the other, rise as they extend north to allow for larger windows on that side of the property.

Under the lower roof, on the south side of the house, one pavilion holds three bedrooms and two bathrooms—what the architects call the "sleeping/private" spaces. Under the more dramatic, higher roof on the north side are the double-height "living/public" areas: a combined living room and kitchen, which opens onto a broad deck on the west and north sides of the house, and a large master bedroom. A hallway running along the house's precise east-west axis unites the two pavilions.

"The bushland experience is central to the design," says Fred Ward, another of the firm's principals. The temperate climate, generally with warm summers and mild (if wet) winters, means that sliding aluminum-framed glass doors in the living room and the master bedroom can be kept open for much of the year. That allows immediate access to the outdoors, where the clients have planted only native species.

From the inside looking out, the drama of the views is heightened by the use of an unassuming palette of materials in the main living and dining space: pale hardwood floors, neutral carpeting, and plasterboard painted off-white, along with joinery and contemporary furniture made from recycled Tasmanian timbers. The result is a space that draws one's attention immediately outward through the trees and bush to the water. A similar respect for the site led to choices of materials on the exterior facade, from oiled timber cladding to deep gray paint for the steel. The house sits in harmony with the remote setting without apologizing for its contemporary profile.

While the architects are happy to take credit for leading the client to accept a long list of green features, there was one battle they admit they lost. Originally, says third principal Mike Verdouw, the firm designed a walking route from a parking

← The way the house is aligned to take advantage of summer shade and winter sun can be easily discerned from its dramatically sweeping roof and deep overhangs.

← Porches, a key amenity in Tasmania's mild climate, are directly accessible from the double-height living room. Thin steel columns and vertical members echo the site's slender eucalyptus trees.

area set roughly 100 yards from the house, so that the first-time visitor would follow a prescribed "sequence of arrival, entry, and discovery of the building" in the trees. But the clients balked, insisting that they be able to drive their cars right up to the edge of the house.

Even in remote Tasmania, apparently, and even when it comes to clients who are clearly committed to sustainability, the lesson is the same as it might be in Los Angeles or a suburb of Atlanta: don't mess with the driveway.

↑ The living room uses pale hardwood floors and neutral carpeting to draw the eye through the windows toward the view of trees and the water surrounding the island of Bruny.

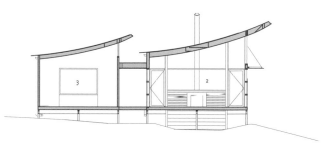

Section

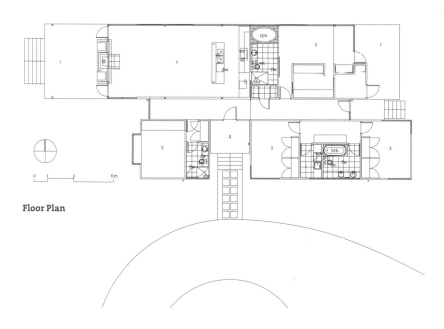

Floor Plan

1 Outdoor living room
2 Living room
3 Sleeping room
4 Entry

McKinley House

LOCATION
Venice, California

ARCHITECTURAL FIRM
David Hertz Architects/Syndesis

DESIGNERS
David Hertz and Stacy Fong

YEAR
2004

David Hertz calls it "McKinley 2.0."

The Southern California architect runs a firm called Syndesis that is well known for its sustainable design expertise and for developing a "green" concrete called Syndecrete. He first designed a 2,400-square-foot house for himself and his family in 1996 in Venice, California, which he dubbed the McKinley House after the street on which it sits, just a stone's throw from the Pacific Ocean. Since then, his family has expanded—he and his wife now have three children between the ages of eight and twelve—and after a while he decided maybe the house needed expanding too. Luckily enough, the property directly north of the existing house became available. Hertz bought it and found himself with a lot that had precisely doubled in size, from 40-by-90 feet to 80-by-90 feet.

← The pool house features doors of certified, sustainably harvested mahogany that slide on custom-designed tracks, allowing nearly the entire ground floor to be opened to the outdoors. Solar panels hidden on the roof heat the pool itself.

Hertz's original design for the house featured two separate volumes: one holding the main residence and the other, a ground-level garage below children's bedrooms, with the two boxes linked by a second-story bridge and passageway. In designing an addition, he decided to extend that theme of separate, smallish structures, each with its own use, and created two new buildings on the new lot. By pushing them to the periphery of the property, he opened up space in between for a semi-enclosed courtyard.

The result, which Hertz says was inspired by Indonesian architecture and is executed in a style that might be called Balinese Modern, with mahogany stairs and trellises, is a compound made up of four discrete two-story buildings linked by three enclosed bridges. All four structures face onto the courtyard, which now includes a thin lap pool with its own open-air shower. On the exterior the buildings feature rough, poured-in-place concrete walls. On the interior courtyard side, they are covered with cast concrete that is smooth and polished enough to be nearly reflective.

One of the new buildings holds a play room on the ground floor and two bedrooms for the kids on the upper story; it is connected to the original children's bedroom above the garage by a glass-enclosed breezeway, which means that a new "children's axis" now runs along the eastern edge of the property on the second story. The second new building holds a pool house with a studio above, which can also be used as a guest house for visitors or even, as Hertz puts it, "for a garage band once the kids get a little older." It is connected to the kids' building by a third bridge that echoes the bridge linking the two parts of the original house and includes a second-floor bathroom designed to glow, like a lantern floating above the ground, at night.

There was only one snag in the whole process, Hertz says. As an architect who thinks of himself as a staunch proponent of green design, the mere fact of adding that much space, however much his family needed it, nagged at him. "There's no getting around the fact," he says, "that on a purely ecological level 4,400 square feet is a lot of house by most of the world's standards."

His solution was to try to make it the greenest house of its size he'd ever seen. "I employ green techniques in all my work," he says, "but I've thought of my own house—both the original and now this addition—as a kind of case study, even a working laboratory, for me to live with environmental systems, materials, and methodologies."

An array of twenty solar panels on the roof generates about 70 percent of the house's energy needs. Other sections of the roof are given over to flat-plate collectors that provide hot water to the water heater, which then sends it into the concrete floors as part of a radiant heating system. Additional hot water is provided by vacuum tubing on the roof, which uses a parabolic collector to focus the sun's rays. All the wood used in the house has been sustainably harvested, and much

↖↖ Hertz used certified epe, a tropical hardwood, on the balcony railings.

↖ The same wood makes up the slats that help shade the breezeway running along the length of the new wing.

←← The ground floor reuses an existing foundation slab as a finish floor, negating the need for additional flooring.

← Natural light is abundant in the top floor of the pool house, which includes a "frameless" skylight above the stair and windows placed to maximize natural ventilation.

↑ The combined living-dining room is hidden from the street by a poured-in-place concrete slab, but light, air, and a sliver of palm-tree view are brought in by operable clerestory windows.

of the concrete is Hertz's own Syndecrete, which contains about 41 percent recycled content and is twice as light, with twice the compressive strength, of normal concrete. The material acts inside the house as a kind of "solar sink" for passive solar energy transfer, storing up the sun's warmth during the day—thus keeping it from overheating the interior—and then slowly releasing that heat during the night.

Hertz hopes that by using Syndecrete in architecturally sophisticated projects like his own residence, he can help speed the adoption of recycled and environmentally friendly products to what he calls "a high-end, design-oriented market segment" that in the past has turned up its nose at green architecture.

He won't be hurt in that effort by the charisma of the house as a whole, which takes full advantage of the balmy coastal climate of Southern California. Wherever possible, Hertz's design blurs the

distinctions between inside and out. "I designed the house in the spirit of architects like Rudolf Schindler, trying to match that manner of living in the California climate, where the building just opens up to the outside," Hertz says. "Being in this climate zone near the ocean allows for a lot of these energy-efficient methodologies to be used."

Indeed, while Hertz says he was careful to keep the literal green-design elements hidden, that strong regional sense helped shape the architecture of the extension as well as the original house, with walkways and sliding doors designed to catch the ocean breezes and the ground-floor rooms flowing seamlessly into the courtyard.

"I always try to make the sustainable elements, even if they're ambitious, subservient to the aesthetic of the architecture," Hertz says. "But you could also say that the way this house responds to the climate became the progenitor of its form."

← The combined living-dining room includes a table made from Syndecrete, a "green" concrete designed by the architect.

↙↙ This detail of a poured-in-place concrete wall shows glass openings that have been cut into it.

↙ The master bedroom, which features radiant in-floor heating and exposed recycled ceiling timbers, opens onto a wraparound balcony.

Exterior Perspective

kitchen

up

bath

pool house

bench

patio

lap pool

dining room

kitchen

existing patio

living room

den

existing garage

rec. room

pool bath

First Floor Plan

terrace balcony

studio

dn

cl.

bathroom

bedroom

loft

cl

bath

line of roof

bedroom

cl

master bedroom

bathroom

sitting rm

bedroom

terrace

office

cl

bedroom

Second Floor Plan

With its often unbearable temperatures

and scarce amounts of natural water, the desert is one of the harshest environments on Earth. But it is also a place of refuge and solace—a sanctuary for people seeking rejuvenation, spiritual uplift, and relief from the crush of big cities. Recently, however, especially in the United States, large tracts of desert land have been metastasizing into suburbs, with homogenous subdivisions connected by six-lane highways.

Deserts cover one-fifth of the Earth's surface, including large swaths of a third of the world's countries, from China, South Asia, the Middle East, and much of Africa to portions of South America, Mexico, and the southwestern United States. They take the form of softly undulating sand dunes, immense arid plains of red clay, crusty salt basins, or rocky mountainous terrain. Where days are defined by punishing heat, temperatures can plummet by up to 70 degrees after the sun sets. Seemingly void, the desert is, in fact, full of life. A rare burst of rainfall can coax a carpet of wild flowers from the cracked dirt that will bloom, seed, and wither in the span of a few days.

Because so many people move to the desert to delight in its natural beauty and dry air, it has been the site of important experiments in sustainable architecture. Yet architecture has no choice but to bend to a climate so extreme, a fact that has given rise to a vernacular architecture based on passive-solar heating and cooling methods and ingenious solutions for ventilation and air-conditioning. The thick walls of an adobe house act as a sponge-like barrier against midday heat; then at night the warmth is released slowly from the walls—an extraordinarily effective means of managing indoor temperatures.

The first consideration in desert architecture is the quantity of space that needs to be kept cool enough for dwelling. Smaller is always better environmentally. But whatever the size, there is also the question of managing the challenges of the intense sun. If a building is longer than it is wide and placed along the track of the sun, then one main wall is protected from direct sunlight. Many desert homes create a cool zone by following this simple rule. Shady interior courtyards, surrounded by the most important rooms of the house, are another tradition in arid settings. Similarly common is a U-shape design, open to the north (or south, depending on the hemisphere), which creates a courtyard in which to enjoy cool evening breezes.

The desert climate is defined not only by temperature fluctuations but by extreme aridity. Less than 10 inches of rainfall a year is typical. Extracting and storing water from deep wells or harvesting rainwater can be surprisingly difficult and expensive—falling rain, for example, must be saved and sealed before it evaporates. Water conservation and planned storage solutions are therefore essential to sustainable desert building. So-called "gray water" systems—which use the same water for more than one function, from washing dishes to landscape irrigation—can drastically reduce water use and consequently, costs. New technologies are becoming available for "cloud harvesting" and "fog catching": common in places like Chile, such systems convert atmospheric moisture into usable water.

Wind, dust, and sand storms are additional menaces. It's crucial to build houses strong enough to withstand them, but that effort is sometimes at odds with a light-on-the-land sustainable ethic. Although the desert does not offer a wide range of local construction materials, environmentally conscious builders try to avoid trucking in large quantities of timber and other materials from faraway sources. Indigenous materials like local stone are better suited to the desert climate, and they blend in better visually.

A host of other architectural solutions can increase the durability and reduce the environmental impact of a desert home: roof overhangs block the high summer sun while allowing in slanted winter rays; a variety of traditional and high-tech materials mimic the elaborately carved screens of South Asian and Middle Eastern houses; narrow windows allow in just enough sun while projecting beautiful streaks of light on the interior walls. The principles involved are rarely new, but they continue to make building in the desert not just possible but rewarding.

TUCSON MOUNTAIN HOUSE

ARCHITECTURAL FIRM
Rick Joy Architects

DESIGNER
Rick Joy

LOCATION
Tucson, Arizona

YEAR
2001

The Tucson Mountain House sits in a secluded valley marked by unusually harsh meteorological extremes. Searing heat alternates with nighttime chills. Monsoon rains crawl up from the south. Thunderstorms appear out of nowhere, electrifying the scrub with lightning bolts. Traditionally, residents in the area have adjusted to the climate by building low-slung adobe dwellings with small windows and thick walls, and much of the area's new construction recalls this classic southwestern regional style. But the earth-colored paint and rounded corners typical of recent subdivisions can't substitute for an authentic vernacular.

Rick Joy, a National Design Award-winning practitioner of environmentally responsible architecture—or "architecture rooted in its place," as he describes it—has put a new spin on time-honored desert building methods. The Tucson-based designer spent twelve years working as a musician and finish carpenter in Maine before enrolling in architecture school at the University of Arizona. After graduating in 1990, he worked for three years in Will Bruder's Phoenix studio before establishing his small, collaborative practice with a series of striated rammed-earth houses that pair ancient building techniques with modern lines and astonishing desert views. All of Joy's projects are driven by a careful consideration of solar orientation and resource conservation. Each one also reflects his profound respect for the landscape and poetic understanding of space. The Tucson Mountain House is a prime example of how the architect's characteristic blend of traditional building techniques, boldly modern shapes, and industrial materials harmonizes with the desert's colors, moods, and topography.

Secluded in the Sonora Desert outside of Tucson, the one-family house for a local couple is deliberately small—less than 2,000 square feet—as if to announce that it cannot possibly compete with the vast mountains looming in the distance or the immense dome of the pitch-black night sky above. Its low profile makes the single-level home unobtrusive in the gently sloping landscape where sagebrush and cacti run rampant.

The house consists of a master bedroom and a guest room adjacent to a combined kitchen-dining-living room. On the north side, a large porch functions as an outdoor room. To the east, a stepped entryway leads down to the foyer. "One of my rules is no garages," Joy says, so the parking area is hidden behind the house and a simple path, aligned axially with the central spine of the house, paves the way to the front door. The compact arrangement has an angular, butterfly-shaped roof of corrugated steel. Its deep eaves shade expansive glass walls that face north and east, offering unobstructed views out to the desert without excessive solar gain. In the other directions, small, geometric cutouts frame the owners' favorite desert vistas. Throughout the house, windows positioned close to ground-level promote cross ventilation.

Ranging from deep rust to pale taupe (depending on the direction and angle of the sun), Joy's signature rammed-earth walls—a mixture of desert soil from the building site and 3-percent Portland cement—endow the Tucson Mountain House with the colors and textures of the surrounding landscape. Poured into wood casts and tamped down in layers, the compound appears striated when it hardens and is removed from the mold, as if eons of geological shifts had formed it. On the exterior, the rammed earth's rough, porous surface blends into the terrain. Inside, where a coating of sealer prevents it from dusting off, its coarseness makes an impressive contrast with the smooth polished concrete floors and minimalist built-in furnishings made of maple. Environmentally, these earthen walls—which run 2 feet thick and 16 feet high on the north and south sides of the house—make an ideal match for the desert by providing passive air-conditioning. Their mass easily absorbs daytime heat, when 100–degree

← Set in the Sonora Desert on a site far removed from the city, Rick Joy's Tucson Mountain House is designed to blend into the landscape, both aesthetically and environmentally.

← On the north side of the house, beneath one wing of the pitched roof, an expansive porch with fireplace, lounge, and views functions as an outdoor room.

temperatures are not uncommon, so that the interior remains cool. At night, when outside temperatures plummet, the walls gradually transfer the stored-up heat, warming the interior.

Like other desert dwellings built by Joy in recent years, the Tucson Mountain House is designed and constructed with a great deal of reverence for the fragile Sonoran ecosystem, a spare, forbidding environment that, on close inspection, brims with many varieties of flora and fauna. Humble yet visually confident, the house satisfies its owners' needs while intruding only minimally on its surroundings. "My version of environmentalism is about a deep level of respect for the landscape," says Joy. "That translates into how I build and what I build. The desert is always the first consideration."

→ The front door, a glass panel set between the stucture's two volumes, offers a first glimpse of the house's stunning desert views.

← ← A wall of east-facing glass panels in the living-dining area opens the house to the desert's rich flora and wildlife.

← In the bathroom, sliding glass doors and mirrored panels create the illusion of an outdoor shower.

↙ ↙ The striated rammed-earth walls supply structure as well as texture, inside and out.

↙ While the house has many large swaths of glass, only a few panels contain operable windows. All of these are strategically positioned to encourage cross ventilation.

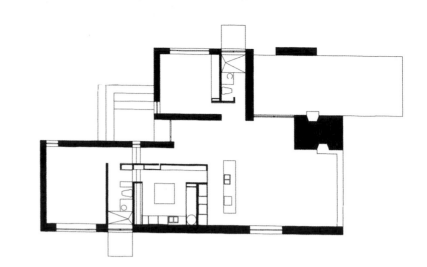

Floor Plan

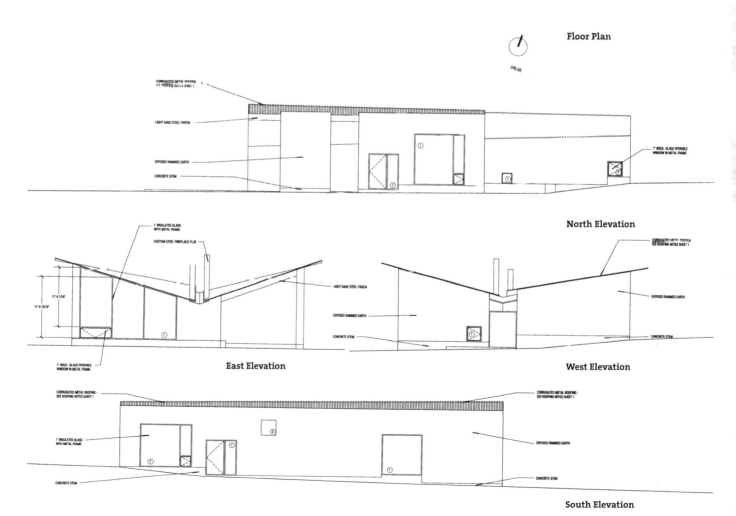

North Elevation

East Elevation

West Elevation

South Elevation

GILES LOFT/STUDIO

LOCATION
San Antonio, Texas

ARCHITECTURAL FIRM
Lake/Flato Architects

DESIGNERS
Ted Flato, Bob Harris, Heather DeGrella

YEAR
2001

No matter how energy-efficient a new structure may be, from the standpoint of ecological impact almost nothing beats a successful effort at saving a building from the wrecking ball. A renovated, low-slung 1920s industrial building in the edgy "Irish Flats" section of San Antonio became a case study in adaptive reuse after surviving a close call with a demolition crew not once, but twice.

Purchased in 1996 by Jill Giles, a local graphic artist, the abandoned warehouse was in the final stages of being converted into a live-work loft space by San Antonio-based Lake/Flato Architects when a welding spark set off a fire. The blaze obliterated most of the architects' renovation work as well as the original wood support structure and part of the roof. When the fire engines rolled out, not much was left other than a stark quadrangle of brick veneer and concrete walls.

Undeterred, Giles and project architect Bob Harris, a partner at Lake/Flato, together with principal-in-charge Ted Flato and Heather DeGrella, decided to make the most of an unexpected turn of events. After nearly a year of construction delays and fights with the insurance company, the design team went back to the drawing board and transformed the burned-out shell into an open-plan loft that puts few demands on the environment and the owner's pocketbook thanks to a spare aesthetic, the deft use of local materials, and a saw-tooth roof that floods the space with natural light.

Named Firm of the Year in 2004 by the American Institute of Architects, Lake/Flato established its practice building environmentally sensitive structures—mainly in rural Texas—that combine the pragmatic solutions of the vernacular with the honesty of modernism. Their sleek, no-nonsense residences and public buildings employ the visual palette of the Southwest without falling victim to frontier nostalgia.

"While writing my college thesis, which was about green design, I came to the conclusion that sustainable building is not so much about what we build as where we build," says Harris. "This house is on the edge of downtown in what could be considered a marginalized area. Just by redoing one derelict space and putting a conscientious person in there, the whole area will begin to improve."

Occupied since 2002, the building is now a live-work space consisting of two large brick structures—each about 4,200 square feet—connected by a gated courtyard. Part of the property's initial appeal for Giles was the promise of eliminating her commute. The site offered plenty of room for both domestic and professional spaces—enough to keep them well separated—plus extra space to lease out for additional income.

In the residential building, a set of large, barn-style rolling doors separates the bedroom and private quarters from the main living space. For the kitchen, Harris designed low-cost custom-made steel cabinets and concrete countertops. He fashioned the dining alcove from one of the only parts of the structure left intact after the fire—a steel box that once housed seismic instruments and other industrial machinery. Tucked into the loft's back corner, the box's warped and buckled walls had taken on a sinuous texture from the heat of the flames. By opening up the box to the main room, the design team created a riveting contrast between the rusted steel and the smooth finish of the surrounding plaster walls. The addition of an old window, salvaged from a warehouse in Austin, made a natural complement.

Between the domestic space and the office space, a courtyard, shielded from neighborhood activity by a 10-foot concrete wall, offers a placid urban retreat. With potted plants, an outdoor fireplace, and a lap pool (modeled on the pool in artist Donald Judd's minimalist compound in Marfa, Texas) the courtyard breathes life into the house and humanizes the industrial aesthetic.

The interior walls of the studio in the adjacent building are veneered in black chalkboard to provide a surface for notes and drawings for the benefit of Giles, her graphic design colleagues, and the staff of the film production company that leases part of

← In keeping with this building's industrial origins, Lake/Flato replaced the fire-damaged ceiling with a saw-tooth roof. From the north end facing south, there appears to be nothing but sky overhead.

↑ Black-painted concrete
fiberboard (a sturdy blend of
recycled paper, cement, and
concrete) set into the original
brick structure preserves the
building's industrial character
from the outside, while ensuring
privacy and security for the
owner on the inside.

the space. Within the open-plan arrangement, a mezzanine loft, accessed by a galvanized-steel staircase, allows for discrete work areas on two levels. The east building's pitched steel support structure, a kind of internal skeleton added after the fire, enables hot air to rise and dissipate. High-efficiency air-conditioning units are required only to regulate the temperature in the bottom half of the space.

Because of the massive saw-tooth roof (inspired, ironically, by an old Friedrich air conditioner factory nearby), Giles's living space receives abundant light. The north-facing clerestory windows in each pitched bay flood the space with a soft, filtered glow. From the south end facing north, the windows appear to form a contiguous opening to the sky. Additional light enters through glass doors that open onto the courtyard as well as through a band of windows coated with tiny ceramic beads that disfuse the light. Positioned high on the

northern and eastern walls, these narrow exposures offer light without sacrificing privacy. "You simply never need to turn on a light in there during the day, even when it's gray and rainy," Harris says. For a complex of this size, that means huge energy savings, since lights are the leading source of energy use in most homes.

For Harris, the house is a testament to Lake/Flato's particular brand of low-impact architecture—an approach to sustainable design that emphasizes low cost, low maintenance, and often seat-of-the-pants solutions that save energy and construction costs by avoiding unnecessary waste and replication: "We're discovering that there's a divide between hardcore environmental technologists—people working toward LEED certifications and using high-tech materials and systems—and people doing smart, thoughtful, local design. The firm works on both fronts, but this house definitely falls into the latter category."

The warm, tobacco-colored patina of the floors makes his case. It was the result of rubbing the fire-damaged cement with old crank-case oil from a local lube shop, a technique that the team had discovered on another project because "it sounded like a good idea," Harris says. Finished with wax, the process is a resourceful alternative to toxic chemical concrete stains.

From the courtyard walls of unfinished concrete block, to the low-grade quarter-inch plywood walls, to the locally produced galvanized stair treads that cost about one dollar each, Lake/Flato's renovation focused on cleaning up and securing the building with the smallest amount of materials and finishes. "We wanted to leave it spare," Harris says. "That's another way to be more environmentally friendly—just put less stuff in it. Fewer elements translate into more flexibility. This building could be easily transformed again someday. That's the most efficient way to build."

→ The site plan illustrates the arrangement of home and work spaces in the two buildings as well as the courtyard and pool between them.

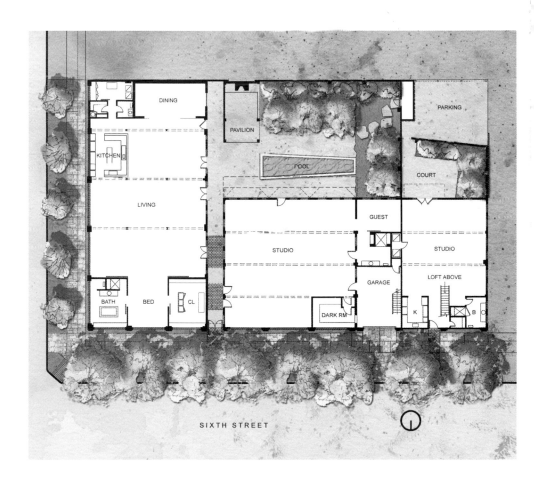

↑→ In the courtyard between the residential building and the office space, a sculptural lap pool helps to cool passing breezes and to offset the compound's urban austerity.

HIGH-EFFICIENCY AIR-CONDITIONING
Because the peaked roof allows hot air to rise, less air conditioning is needed and then, only on the hottest days.

FRITTERED GLASS
Covered with small ceramic dots that act like light-transmitting blinds, the windows and skylights reduce heat gain and glare while keeping the space bright.

PLASTER WALLS
With a high sand content, the plaster walls act as thermal collectors, aborbing much of the heat so that the air temperature stays cool.

SAW-TOOTH ROOF
The north-facing glass panels flood the house with light. Even on gray days, artificial light is rarely necessary.

LOLOMA 5 LOFTS

ARCHITECTURAL FIRM
Will Bruder Architects

DESIGNER
Will Bruder

LOCATION
Scottsdale, Arizona

YEAR
2004

The dry, hot city of Scottsdale, known for its false-fronted, Old-West architecture and as a home for spring-training baseball, is located just northeast of Phoenix in the urbanized Sonora Desert. The city didn't have any kind of municipal green-building program when Will Bruder, one of the Southwest's leading architects, began work on an extension to the Scottsdale Museum of Contemporary Art in the mid-1990s. His scheme for the museum, which turned an old art-house movie theater into gallery space and draped its exterior in various kinds of galvanized steel, was eye-catching and popular when it opened in 1999, yes. But not green.

By the time another Scottsdale commission, this one residential, came Bruder's way a few years later, the city had put ambitious new sustainability guidelines into place. They call for projects that are small (less than 3,000 square feet for a single-family house, for example), careful to preserve water and other resources (no swimming pools or lawns), and that pay attention to passive-solar strategies (the longest axis of the project must be oriented to face within 20 degrees of due south, and low-emission windows are recommended). Points are also awarded for efficient insulation, non-toxic paints and finishes, and landscaping and driveways that mitigate impact on site topography, among other criteria. Buildings that meet the city's basic requirements receive an Entry Level green rating, while designs that meet more stringent ones are ranked at the Advanced Level.

The guidelines are not prescriptive: they don't require that every bit, or even a set percentage, of new construction in the city meet green benchmarks. But they allow sustainable developments to be put on an expedited approval track, with Advanced Level projects getting the most favorable treatment; they promote green architecture with a carrot instead of a stick. "So you make your choice," Bruder explains. "You do something conventional and go through the old, slow process. Or you do something sustainable and move that much more quickly."

Bruder went for green and for speed. For a lot just four blocks away from the museum, on a street lined with palm trees and low-rise apartment buildings, Bruder and his colleagues at Will Bruder Architects produced a striking collection of five live-work lofts that combine attention to region and sustainability with stripped-down but forceful, even muscular, contemporary form. Each unit of the LoLoma 5 Lofts includes 1,550 square feet on three floors: commercial space on the ground floor topped by two-bedroom, two-story apartments. The building is located in the new Scottsdale Arts District and is within walking distance—at least on a relatively cool day, or in the morning or evening—not just of the museum but of other cultural facilities, restaurants, and mass transit stops. The building qualified for distinction at the Advanced Level of the city's green program.

The green elements begin just past the curb: what the architects call the "auto court" is lined with crushed compacted granite, with no concrete or asphalt. This pavement helps keep temperatures down on a surface that Bruder says "could have been a heat trap" and integrates the building with the surrounding landscape.

The western facade, facing the street, is relatively buttoned up, clad in Rheinzink panels and narrow-gauge windows that direct thin columns of evening light into the kitchens. Also visible from the street is the northern facade, which tells a more complicated story about sustainability in a region where the sun is something both to be treasured—it's the reason most people move to this part of the country, after all—and feared for the damage it can do.

The northern facade features the most glass. But because even December days can be hot here, and because spring and fall are often downright scorching, this side of the building also shows signs of an effort to protect residents from the sun. The

← The exterior of each unit in Will Bruder's LoLoma 5 building includes a balcony cantilevered from the facade to grab views of the desert from two directions. Perforated metal screens help control the level of sunlight inside.

↑↑ The western facade is faced in Rheinzink panels sliced through vertically with narrow windows.

↑ The eastern facade has slightly wider windows.

↗ Parking spaces at the base of the building are accessed via an auto court made with crushed granite instead of asphalt or cement—materials the architect says would have created a heat trap in the desert sun.

windows are substantially covered with perforated metal scrims, which are about 70 percent solid and 30 percent void. The scrims cover the upper half of the second-story windows and most of the windows on the third floor.

The views from inside through the scrims are more transparent than you would guess. And the design does offer plenty of opportunity for residents to step outside at times of the day—and of the year—when the sun is less than intense. Each unit includes a balcony on the second story, cantilevered out from the facade and twisted a bit to grab views to the north and west, where Camelback Mountain rises 900 feet above the desert floor. There is also a roof-top balcony for each loft on the southern side of the building, offering views of the city, the desert, and the Sandstone Papago Buttes, as well as a cool place to sleep on warm nights. "We wanted to recapture the whole spirit of sleeping porches," Bruder says, citing Rudolf Schindler's own 1922 house in Hollywood as an inspiration. The architect says that both balconies are designed to provide "outdoor living environments that accommodate the sun's path and this climate we're in."

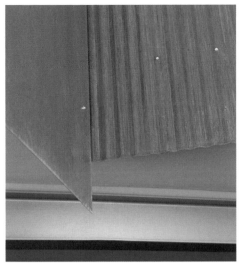

↑ The building includes a palette of materials inspired, Bruder says, by everything from the color of the desert floor to Frank Lloyd Wright's nearby Taliesen West.

Inside, the lofts are open and airy. Bruder estimates that the ventilation system will allow residents to use natural cooling for much of the year. Most residential buildings in the area close off to the elements rather than try to engage them, as Bruder's does. "I don't think most people here who live in row-house units like these are used to the ability to open and close the windows and bring ventilation all the way through the house," he says. He estimates that from the middle of September to the middle of May residents will be able to live essentially without air-conditioning, reducing to four the months of the year when they will have to rely heavily on artificial cooling.

Despite their great views and striking architecture, the units in the LoLoma project are not extravagant. Bruder says he prefers working with tight spaces, where every square foot counts. He says the finished lofts "have a sailboat modesty to them—everything in its place—that breeds an attitude of efficiency."

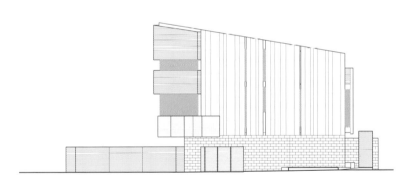

West Elevation

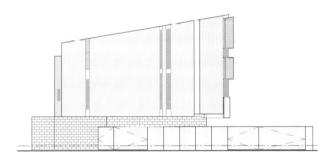

East Elevation

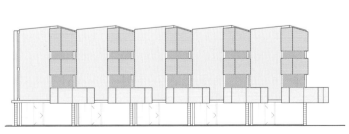

North Elevation

South Elevation

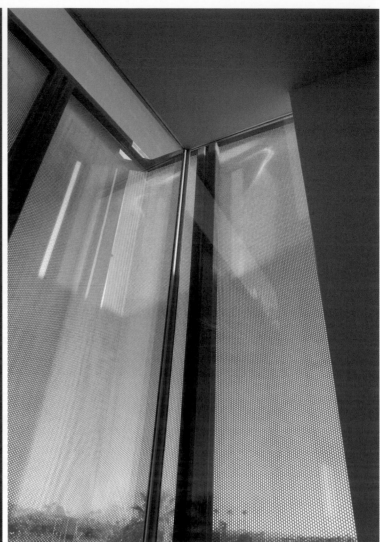

↑↗ The windows on the northern side of the building are partially enclosed inside perforated metal screens that help reduce glare and solar gain. Seen from inside, the screens maintain a surprising degree of transparency.

↖|↑ Windows deliver thin columns of light into the kitchen and offer expansive views from the bedroom.

← Roof balconies are tucked away on the southern side of the building and can be used as sleeping porches.

Between the Tropic of Cancer and the

Tropic of Capricorn lies a region where there are just two seasons and temperatures are persistently high. The oppressive heat and humidity give way to periods of epic rainfall and punishing storms—typhoons, cyclones, tornadoes—that can cause indiscriminate damage whenever and wherever they strike.

At other times, the tropics exude a tranquility that has no match elsewhere on the planet, offering a soft, sweet, and lush refuge of emerald forests and turquoise oceans that is aptly described as paradise. Almost 40 percent of the Earth's land surface falls between these two latitudes and about a third of the world's population lives there, often under chronic economic deprivation. Millions more arrive annually for short visits, spurred by an ever more ambitious and far-flung tourism industry.

"If there is one thing that characterizes life in the tropics, it is the ability to live in close contact with the exterior environment and enjoy the sensation of openness and closeness to nature this brings," writes Bruno Stagno in his book *An Architect in the Tropics*. The tropics demand adaptability from both inhabitants and the structures in which they live. Indigenous populations have been practicing green architecture for countless generations, harnessing trees for their cool shade or the sea breeze for its free and consistant ventilation—the central necessity of tropical architecture. Thatching and woven leaves serve as fans and as protection against rain. High-pitched roofs deflect the wind; jack roofs (elevated clerestory openings) enhance cross ventilation and allow heat to escape quickly. Heavy but flexible bamboo frames resist earthquakes and high winds. Terraces, canopies, blinds, covered verandas, and wide overhanging eaves block direct sunlight. Stilts and slatted floors protect against water damage and heat exposure. All these vernacular solutions reappear in the high-tech designs of contemporary green architects working in the tropics.

Environmentally conscious tropical architecture must also tackle logistical and technical problems that do not exist in the same combination elsewhere: from bio-deterioration and excess rainwater, to pest and fungal infestation, to the limited availability of natural building materials. Planning for a fully integrated indoor-outdoor lifestyle is essential. Special consideration must be given to reducing glare and maximizing shade but also to protecting against hurricane winds, floods, landslides, earthquakes, and severe lightning.

Meteorologically, what distinguishes the tropics from other regions the most is humidity. Although it contributes to a vast and easily harnessed water supply, humidity gives rise to specific construction problems. Of particular concern is the accelerated rate at which organic materials decompose. Soil erosion creates special engineering challenges when it comes to designing foundations that will withstand severe weather. Humidity also makes it harder to balance structural stability with environmental sensitivity. To protect against virulent corrosion, for example, metal should be treated with rust-resistant agents, but such treatments are usually toxic and high in volatile organic compounds. The same is true for treatments commonly used on wood to protect against both weather and insect infestation, which can pose a serious threat to any tropical building.

In our era of rampant deforestation, when hundreds of acres of tropical rainforests are clear-cut every day, the use of sustainably harvested or fast-growth timber has never been more crucial. When the tropical canopy is destroyed, animal species that rely on trees for food and habitat suffer—and half of the globe's living species are said to be found only in tropical environments. By minimizing reliance on non-sustainable timber, architects can act responsibly in the face of these threats. Similar responses are required to counteract the alarming destruction of coral reefs, from the Florida Keys to Australia's Great Barrier Reef. Architects can help prevent further deterioration of reefs—which, like underwater rainforests, host a rich diversity of aquatic species—by limiting the use of toxic building materials and incorporating environmentally sound water and sewage treatment systems.

Though these are serious concerns for architecture in tropical regions, the beauty and serenity of tropical life can be preserved with careful long-range planning and construction. The vernacular architecture of the tropics has provided a wellspring of inspiration for contemporary green architects, who are now in the position to return the favor.

CASUARINA BEACH HOUSE

LOCATION
Kingscliff, New South Wales, Australia

ARCHITECTURAL FIRM
Lahz Nimmo Architects

DESIGNERS
Annabel Lahz and Andrew Nimmo

YEAR
2001

The ultimate beach house: for some it's a tiny thatched hut with a hammock and a surfboard; for others it's a Gatsby-esque pile. For Annabel Lahz and Andrew Nimmo, it's a contemporary study in indoor/outdoor living that is built to be as comfortable for the local ecosystem as it is for its inhabitants.

↑ The compact, battened-down facade of Lahz Nimmo's Casuarina Beach House forms a striking contrast to its expansive, lofty interior spaces, which open wide to the surrounding dunes.

← Slatted timber cladding and louvered windows help keep breezes flowing throughout the "sleeping box," one of two discrete structures that comprise the house.

Lahz Nimmo Architects, the partners' ten-year-old Sydney-based practice, was one of fourteen firms invited to participate in a competition to come up with the perfect spec home for a piece of ocean-front property on the Pacific near Kingscliff, in the blustery tropics of northern New South Wales. Organized by Australian developer Consolidated Properties, the "Ultimate Beach House" contest proved to be an efficient way for the company to both develop and promote its new project at Casaurina Beach. Lahz Nimmo's handsome, horizontally clad house was one of three winning designs and the first to be built on the site, a rejuvenated former sand mine. Self-sufficient and smartly stylish, it set the standard for quality design in the new development and served as a prototype for testing the marketability of "Sustainable House Packages" there. Consolidated's president Donald O'Roark, a "mad keen surfer," as Nimmo describes him, thought the project so successful, he bought the house himself.

Set back about 350 feet behind the dunes, amid the ubiquitous casuarina trees after which the beach was named, the house cuts a long, linear profile. Two rectangular volumes connected by a double-height breezeway comprise the interior space. The open-plan living pavilion on the east side of the site extends out toward the sand and sea with a retractable glass wall on one side and floor-to-ceiling windows on the other. Floating over the landscape on steel struts, it contains kitchen, dining, and lounge areas under a soaring, single-pitch roof. The two-story timber "sleeping box," which contains three bedrooms, three bathrooms, a garage, and a "rumpus room," is, by contrast, firmly anchored to the ground and more shielded from the elements by a series of glass louvers and wood battens. The reason for separating the two structures has to do with "zoning," says Nimmo. "We were thinking about how beach holidays work, how there are always extra people around, and came up with this two-part structure as a way of allowing different groups and different activities to coexist happily."

In the spaces between and around the two buildings, the architects found room for a private garden courtyard, an extensive lawn, a covered veranda, a vast open-air deck, and a compact plunge pool. "The winds can be pretty full-on sometimes and they tend to change direction depending on the season," says Nimmo, so the different types and locations of outdoor spaces were designed to "ensure that at any time of the year or day, there will always be one perfect place to be comfortable outside the house."

Throughout the property, Lahz and Nimmo used materials that would stand up to the wind and salt without impinging on the environment. They chose blue gum, a native hardwood, salvaged from an old railway bridge, for the battens and cladding. It was more expensive than new timber, but "because builders tended to use mature trees back then, the color and grain are much more stable than what you can find now," Nimmo explains. The wood is treated only with oil, which preserves its rich color and protects against UV rays.

While they were conscious of minimizing the amount of metal in the house, since it has to be so heavily treated to avoid corrosion in the salty air, the architects did incorporate hot-dipped galvanized steel for the support trusses and aluminum for the window frames. Because heat loss is not a problem, thanks to the region's mild, tropical weather, they selected standard glass, but protected all exposures with shady overhangs or timber battens to reduce solar gain.

As a result of the wide array of ecologically sustainable design solutions incorporated into the plan, the house requires virtually no resources it cannot generate on its own. Photovoltaic panels

↑↑ When the living room's wall-size door is retracted, the whole pavilion takes on the feel of one big veranda.

↑ The house's two discrete sections—living pavilion to the left, sleeping box to the right—are linked by a low-slung breezeway.

↑↑ The covered breezeway joining the two pavilions functions as a thermal chimney, coaxing hot air up and out while drawing in cool air from below.

↑ Open and covered decks, patios, and verandas fan out in every direction, allowing for outdoor activities regardless of wind direction or season.

on the roof produce electricity for the energy-efficient appliances. When the house is at maximum capacity, it may draw power from the electrical grid, but at other times the cells generate enough power to earn back credits from the local utility. The extensive water-recycling program includes a purifying system that transforms rain into drinking water and waste water into irrigation and flushing water. Sewage and storm water never leave the site—they're treated in a series of gravel-lined cisterns—and no fresh water is imported. (Municipal water is available, but only as a backup in case of a drought.)

There is no air-conditioning system, either. The breezeway connecting the two parts of the house functions as a thermal chimney that draws in the cool ocean breezes at the bottom and expels hot air out the top. Shutters and louvers regulate the amount of light and air entering the building. When the sun is high, the shades can be positioned to deflect the harsh rays without blocking all of the light or air. "The first time I went for a visit after it was built, it was a stinking hot day," Nimmo remembers, "but when I walked inside, it was beautifully cool, yet flooded with light. That's the best thing about this house—it breathes."

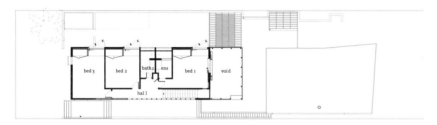

Second Floor Plan

First Floor Plan

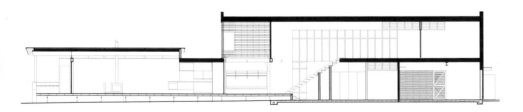

Section

RECLAIMED WOOD CLADDING
All exterior timber cladding and battens are of blue gum, a hardwood native to the area that the architects salvaged from an old railway bridge. The hoop-pine plywood ceiling panels were sourced from plantation timbers.

NO-TECH VENTING
Despite the tropical conditions, the house contains no mechanized air-conditioning aside from ceiling fans. Slatted panels above doorways allow for cross ventilation at night.

FOUNDATION-LESS STRUCTURE
Elevated on treated steel struts (not shown), the house hovers over the landscape instead of being set into the earth. This arrangement not only minimizes the environmental impact, it also allows cool air to circulate up from underneath.

ON-SITE WATER PURIFICATION
A series of cisterns converts rain into drinking water and treats waste water for use in irrigation and flushing so that neither storm water nor sewage ever leaves the site.

TAYLOR HOUSE

ARCHITECTURAL FIRM
Frank Harmon and Associates

DESIGNER
Frank Harmon

LOCATION
Scotland Cay, Bahamas

YEAR
2001

From a distance, it looks like a cartoon: a crisp, boxy beach house with distinct echoes of Bauhaus modernism that's gone on a madcap spree—its windows are flapping, its doors are flailing, its decks are spread akimbo, and its pyramid-shaped roof appears to have popped up into the air, done a somersault, and landed back on the house with its pointy end facing down.

← To protect against the ferocious winds and epic rains that regularly hit the Bahamas, architect Frank Harmon designed a series of doors and hatches for the Taylor house that can be battened down as soon as the clouds roll in. When the skies are clear, the open flaps function as a low-tech ventilation system that keeps the whole house full of cool off-shore breezes.

When the late industrial designer Jim Taylor began to think about a vacation house for himself and his wife, Janice, in the lush Bahaman hideaway of Scotland Cay, he knew it wouldn't be a typical home. The inventor of the first bar-code reading machine, Taylor was an innovator who always searched for unorthodox solutions to whatever puzzle he was working on (an earlier home of his, in Raleigh, North Carolina, featured rooms on air cushions that could be moved around freely). The remote spot he picked for the couple's new seaside house certainly offered challenges that would have been a deterrent to some homebuilders: though postcard-perfect from a photographer's vantage point, the Abaco Islands are full of tropical dangers, from blistering sun and swarms of scorpions to category-five hurricanes that emerge from out of nowhere and rip out whole clusters of mahogany trees.

To cope with these and other local problems, including the absence of fresh water, the Taylors turned to Frank Harmon, a Raleigh-based architect. Some of the design decisions seemed obvious. The house would have to be relatively tall, for example, not only for the views but so that the living quarters could rise above the mosquito line. Natural ventilation would have to suffice for air-conditioning. Other complexities called for more ingenuity. The biggest problem was the lack of fresh water on the island, which meant that rainwater would have to be collected for drinking, cooking, washing, and bathing.

Harmon's masterstroke—an inverted "umbrella" roof clad with marine plywood and native pine on its underside—solved several design problems at once, while adding a signature architectural element to the house. The 6-inch steel pipe in the bottom of the funnel-like roof directs harvested rainwater through the house and down into an 8,000-gallon cistern at ground level. It provides plenty of water for all the household needs plus extra stores for emergencies. Meanwhile, the sprawling eaves offer welcome shade and circulate cool ocean breezes in the third-floor open-plan living dining room and kitchen, which offers majestic views of the turquoise ocean and a sense of living directly under the sky. "The constant flow of fresh air makes this a very healthy home," says Harmon. "And, to me, that's the number one goal. Why else would you make a green house?"

The upside-down roof is both visually striking and functionally important. But it took Harmon some time to figure out how to keep it from flying off if hit with one of the area's frequent tropical storms, which often come with wind speeds of up to 100 miles per hour. Following the lead of structural engineer Greg Sullivan, Harmon tethered the roof's steel skeleton to four concrete columns that are connected directly to the foundation.

Additional logistical issues had to be overcome in the process of construction. The crew, working without a crane, would have to do all the heavy lifting by hand. Non-indigenous materials could play only a minimal role, since everything had to be shipped in on boats. In fact, the steel beams accounted for the only building material that did not come from within a 20-mile radius. The exterior is composed of readily available reinforced concrete blocks, wood, and stucco. On the interior, Harmon utilized one of the island's most abundant resources: coral. Both the interior and exterior floors, as well as the kitchen counters, are made from slabs of a soft, pink limestone-like coral that was excavated from the foundation hole and is naturally embedded with tiny ancient sea shells.

Much of the effort during both the design and construction phases went into creating a system of shutters, flaps, and rolling doors that can be

↑ Pitched downward beneath a flat topline, the angled roof is designed to collect rainwater and then funnel it down to an 8,000-gallon cistern.

← To reduce exposure to insects, one of the island's main hazards, Harmon elevated the main living space and cleared the brush around the base of the house.

→ Like nearly all the materials used in the house, the wood cladding on the underside of the roof's wide eaves was harvested locally.

battened down to brace the house against gale-force winds. In good weather, the sliding panels and flip-up shutters, which are reinforced with stainless steel and Plexiglas and painted in Caribbean shades of light blue and pastel yellow, open out in every direction, lending the house an air of whimsy. But when storms approach, the house goes into lockdown mode. Thanks to this sturdy system of panels, the Taylor house survived Hurricane Floyd, which devastated many nearby homes and left the normally emerald-green island a pale shade of brown—even the grass had been ripped out of the earth.

Perched on a coral ridge 30 feet high and about 200 feet from the shore break, the beach house follows many of the key principles of sustainable design—adapting to the local climate, making use of naturally available resources, deploying low-impact air-conditioning technologies, and minimizing long-haul transportation and disruption to the native landscape. "We were very careful not to disturb anything during construction," says Harmon. But he does admit to cutting down poisonwood trees (because they are toxic) and to replacing the brush right around the house with a sort of white sand moat (because it's a good method of deterring bugs and scorpions)—two harmless ways of ensuring a friendly environment for the house's inhabitants.

Harmon tried to make the house as self-sufficient as possible. Its two bedrooms are on the middle, or "tree-top," level, as Harmon calls it, where the stair landing leads onto a 48-foot-long deck facing due west out over the Sea of Abaco.

From the cantilevered balcony outside the master bedroom, Janice Taylor can reach out and pick a papaya right off the tree. Other tropical edibles grown on the half-acre property include coconuts, key limes, grapefruits, and oranges. On the ground level, which is accessed via a winding, orchid-lined footpath, a large, bunker-like workshop accounts for the remainder of the house's 3,000-square-foot living quarters (only 1,500 of which are indoors). "The first rule of the Bahamas is that everything breaks, so each house has to have a workshop," says Harmon. "It's a place where people become really resourceful. There are no shops, no doctors, no organized entertainments whatsoever. It may look like paradise, but it's real. That's why the Taylors chose it. They wanted to live in the environment; they weren't looking for Disneyland."

↑ With only 1,500 square feet of interior space, much of the living at the Taylor house happens outdoors, where another 1,500 square feet of deck space, including this covered terrace off the kitchen, provides room for eating, lounging, and admiring the view of the Abaco Sea.

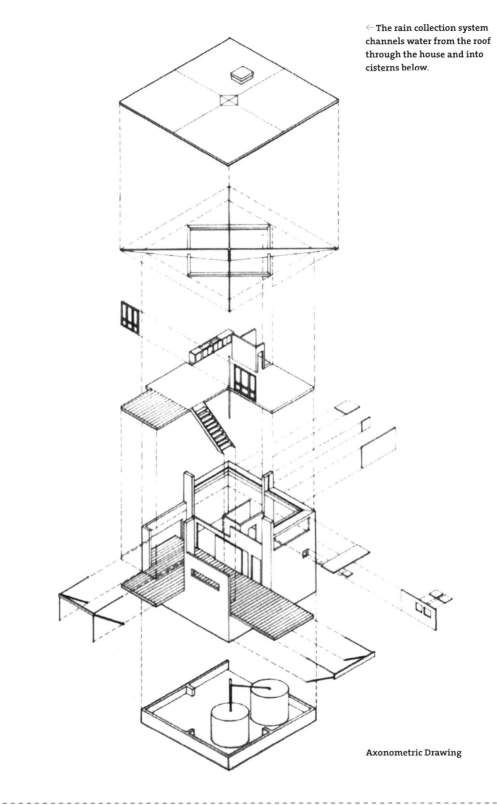

← The rain collection system channels water from the roof through the house and into cisterns below.

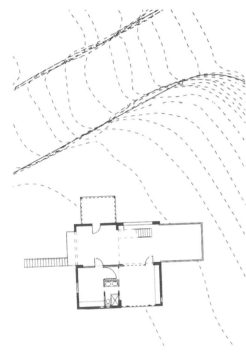

Site Plan

Axonometric Drawing

CASA DE CARMEN

LOCATION
Baja California Sur, Mexico

ARCHITECTURAL FIRM
Leddy Maytum Stacy Architects

DESIGNERS
Marsha Maytum and Roberto Sheinberg

YEAR
2001

Though geographically tropical, Baja California Sur—the southern portion of Mexico's thousand-mile-long peninsula stretching between the Pacific Ocean and the Sea of Cortez—is technically part of the Sonora Desert. Its arid climate and parched terrain appeared like something of an oasis to Carmen Gutierrez and Rodney Bradley, a retired couple from Anchorage. After years of freezing Alaskan winters, Baja's warm Pacific waters and golden, sandy bluffs were just what they had been looking for. So when they spotted a "Land for Sale" sign while cruising off the region's west coast, they didn't hesitate to commit.

← Set between a vast track of tropical desert and the shimmering water of the Pacific Ocean, Leddy Maytum Stacy's Casa de Carmen is designed for both shade and spectacular views.

Part of a new development in an unpopulated area, their lot—a 70-by-250-foot-long swath atop a 20-foot-high bluff facing the Pacific—is twenty minutes from the nearest town. While the property's splendid isolation appealed to the couple as a perfect antidote to their life up north, its consequent lack of utilities—water is available via an aquifer, but there is no infrastructure for gas, oil, or electricity—presented a host of challenges when it came time to build a house.

Gutierrez and Bradley knew Marsha Maytum, a principal of Leddy Maytum Stacy Architects in San Francisco (formerly Tanner Leddy Maytum Stacy), would be up for the job. Maytum was Gutierrez's college roommate and had been a friend ever since. A member of the Green Building Council and of the International Green Building Challenge's U.S. team, Maytum built a practice designing residential and commercial structures—including San Francisco's Thoreau Center for Sustainability—that combine "modern, rational, economic, and sustainable solutions," as she has described them.

Working with project architect Roberto Sheinberg, a native of Mexico City, Maytum responded to the clients' request for "something Mexican and modern." The design's boxy volumes, vibrant colors, and emphasis on gardens and outdoor spaces certainly evoke the work of Mexican modernist Luis Barragán. But its large windows, loft-like spaces, and unconcealed photovoltaic panels also suggest a more contemporary approach.

The couple's requirements were relatively simple: they wanted a second-floor master bedroom facing the ocean, a casual living-dining area, some space for houseguests, and a garden. "We decided to make all the rooms open to the ocean," says Sheinberg, "but also to keep the water views hidden until you enter the house—that way there is an element of surprise, a payoff for the long journey from Alaska."

Composed of two main volumes that break up the elongated site and afford ample wind-protected patio space, the 4,700-square-foot house (including patio and garage) is a reinterpretation of the traditional Mexican courtyard arrangement. A ceremonial entry sequence proceeds from the desert via a slatted-wood gate along a series of paths, through an open-air tower past gardens and patios, and culminating in the shelter of the house and its stunning ocean vistas (which frequently include a pod of majestic California Gray whales that migrate to Baja's warm waters for mating and birthing). To the basic living spaces the architects added a rooftop deck, a terrace off the guest rooms, a covered outdoor dining area, and the tower with its cut-out corner as a quiet reading space. "The tower was important compositionally," says Sheinberg, "but it was also another way to create outdoor space. We felt this house should encourage as much outdoor living as possible."

From the largest forms to the smallest details, the design was based on locally available materials and techniques that the members of the construction crew, who came from a small town on the Mexican mainland, would know how to handle. Mexican stucco—a nearly maintenance-free cement-plaster recipe that is harder and more concrete-like than American stucco—covers the exterior. The thick concrete-block walls, a typically Mexican construct, are in-filled with concrete for extra protection against the heat. The country's ubiquitous blue mosaic tile and blue-gray slate pave the garden walls and paths. Cantera, a pale Mexican stone that looks like limestone but is harder and less porous, adorns the interior floors. All the woodwork—including numerous shutters, gates, and doors—was done on site with available alder wood by local carpenters accustomed to its texture and density.

In every case the architects tried to use what was there and not import from the mainland or the States. This includes all the furniture, which was custom built on site, as well as everything in the gardens. "From the beginning we planned to do a

desert garden," says Sheinberg. "It was always meant to be very dry, using sand from the site. At some point we added a line of cacti, but everything else was found on site."

With no electrical grid to tap into, the house has to generate its own power for everything from heating water to turning on a light. Two 12-by-12-foot photovoltaic panels set in the middle of the garden on a rotating base track the sun for maximum solar gain. So far, Gutierrez and Bradley have not had to resort to the backup generator they keep on hand, even when the house is full of overnight guests. High-efficiency appliances and lighting fixtures help conserve energy. The whole house was designed

to minimize the need for artificial lighting and mechanical air-conditioning: cross ventilation and ceiling fans promote cooling breezes; sun shading at all openings minimizes heat gain; skylights and clerestory windows increase natural light; pale pavers on the roof deck reflect the sunlight and improve heat-gain; and the ocean wall supports a trellis, which provides shade and protects the house during hurricanes.

"We studied all of the ways—both ancient and modern—of keeping the house comfortable," says Sheinberg. "It really helped us understand how to keep the environment comfortable, too."

→ The entry path to the low-slung, concrete and stucco house leads from the slatted gate in the sand-colored wall past the courtyard garden.

↙ A "dry" garden, composed of cacti and other desert flora collected from around the property, forms the centerpiece of the compound.

↓ Wooden slats made from local alder wood form a shady trellis over the patio off the guest room.

Casa de Carmen

↖ Deep red stucco, marine blue mosaic tiles, and a jagged, cantilevered staircase provide a vibrant backdrop to the outdoor dining area.

← The interior palette of red tiles, pale yellow walls, and blue accents mimics the colors used outdoors to extend the sense of living space.

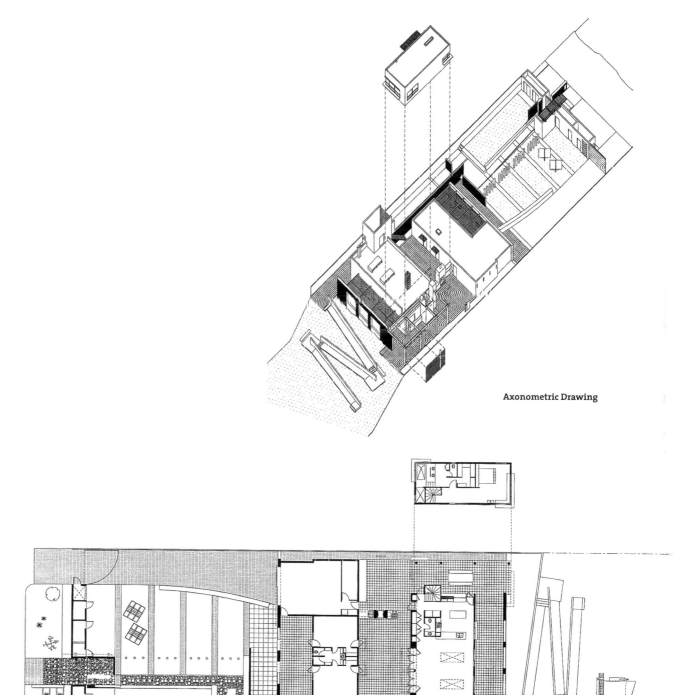

Axonometric Drawing

Site and Floor Plan

One of the most significant

developments in residential architecture over the last several years, particularly in the United States and Europe, has been the effort to rehabilitate the reputation of prefabricated, or modular, housing. Using powerful design software that allows them to combine the cost savings of factory-built homes with the aesthetic benefits of customized design, a number of young firms are creating modular houses that offer sophisticated architecture at a remarkably low price.

It is now becoming possible to pick a design from one of those firms' Web sites, order a house that can be altered specifically to fit your family's needs and the contours of your building site, get the house delivered on the back of a truck, and have it built—all within in a few short months. Perhaps most important of all, these are not the banal tract homes one tends to associate with the term "prefab." Instead, many are sleek and attractive, driven as much by aesthetics as by economy. A significant number are designed in the modernist idiom, which means you can now bring the Bauhaus to your house on an everyman's budget.

Of course, using mass-produced parts and automated design technology to bring well-designed residences to the middle class has been a dream of architects since the beginning of the modern movement. It emerged during the early years of the twentieth century, as European architects predicted that modern building techniques would help liberate families from cramped, decrepit housing, and again in the postwar period, as architects from Jean Prouvé to Buckminster Fuller to Charles and Ray Eames tried to perfect modular residential designs that could be all but erected on an assembly line. Alas, those dreams have been repeatedly dashed by the realities of the building trade, whose leading companies have proved reluctant to change their ways or to test the market for houses with forward-looking, ornament-free design.

This new wave of prefab-modern architects, however, shows significantly more promise than the ones that came before. There are now more than a dozen firms selling "modern modular" designs; many are run by young, ambitious architects who in the past three to four years have displayed more savvy about how the construction industry works than their prefab predecessors ever did. And as the design featured in the following pages, by the California-based architect Michelle Kaufmann, demonstrates, prefab housing and sustainability are well matched. Every prefab design is fundamentally green by definition, at least in the sense that its construction is bound to leave far less debris and do less damage to a building site than a typical new house. And incorporating additional green features, from solar panels to ambitious ventilation systems, is likely to make prefab housing only that much more attractive to environmentally minded buyers.

In a prefab marketplace that is increasingly crowded with attractive designs and featured regularly in the popular and design press, sustainability can be a smart marketing tool too. If this new crop of modular houses achieves its great potential and allows middle-class families to build their own stylish houses quickly and affordably, prefabrication might just become the best delivery system for sustainable design yet.

GLIDE HOUSE

ARCHITECTURAL FIRM
Michelle Kaufmann Designs

DESIGNER
Michelle Kaufmann

LOCATION
Anywhere

YEAR
2004

Among the emerging breed of modernist prefab homes, the first to take an active interest in sustainability is the Glide House, an airy, light-filled design by Michelle Kaufmann, a young architect based in Northern California. Kaufmann spent five years in the office of Frank O. Gehry & Partners before leaving to start her own firm. Working with a modular design company in Washington State and builders in Toronto and Vancouver, Kaufmann has begun selling several variations of the Glide House, ranging from one to four bedrooms and from 672 to 2,016 square feet on one or two stories. The price—including the cost of the design, trucking materials to the site, and construction, but excluding the solar panels on the roof and the appliances in the kitchen—begins at about $120 per square foot for a level lot.

→ The basic Glide House module is an attractively spare single-story residence with sliding glass doors along the length of the southern facade. Solar panels and wind turbines can be added to the roof for an additional fee, allowing buyers of the house to live without connection to the power grid.

That translates to less than $200,000 for most variations, a bargain for a house of this level of architectural quality and attention to detail. Kaufmann built a version of the house for herself and her husband in Northern California in early 2004. A few months later, the first Glide House to be sold was erected in Washington state.

A basic wood-frame construction made of prefabricated panels, the house is "designed for clean, simple living in collaboration with nature," in Kaufmann's words. In the single-story base model, the living areas are contained in one long rectangular room. Beneath a relatively high, gently pitched shed roof, the plan includes a glass wall on one side and a row of clerestory windows on the other, above built-in cabinets with sliding birch doors. Bedrooms and bathrooms are tucked away in an adjacent suite of rooms. The basic modules are 14 or 16 feet wide, which allows them to fit on the back of a flatbed truck for delivery and also makes for shallow rooms that are easily ventilated by cross-breezes.

The house features a significant number of green elements. The prefabricated nature of the design results in comparatively little construction waste, particularly on site. Photovoltaic panels can be ordered to cover a sizable percentage of the roof area. More ambitious homeowners can order a version of the house that uses those panels or wind power, or a combination of the two, to produce enough electricity to remove the house from the grid. That means it can be built even on remote sites that lie beyond the reach of local utilities.

In terms of passive rather than active solar power, Kaufmann will work with clients to position the house on their site to minimize solar loss in the winter and solar gain in the summer. Sliding panels of louvered wood cover the long glass facade; they can be adjusted to control the level of sunlight entering the house while maintaining air flow. These panels can be moved to follow the sun or locked in place even when the glass doors behind them are kept open; that arrangement allows owners to cool their houses on a warm day by circulating air rather than running an air conditioner, even when they have to go out.

The materials and finishes, from bamboo flooring to composite concrete countertops that include recycled newspaper and granite ash, were also chosen with sustainability in mind. The walls and roof are made of structurally insulated panels, or SIPS, a system that is well regarded for its insulation and its resistance to mold. The exterior paneling, a choice of COR-TEN steel or the corrugated metal known as Galvalume, is durable and requires little maintenance.

The sustainable ethic in this remarkable design extends even to the smallest details: the storage cabinets that run beneath the clerestory windows in the living room are topped by reflective panels, placed specifically to bounce late-afternoon sunlight onto the ceiling and back down into the house. This small, studied detail, which helps delay the time of day when it becomes necessary to turn on the lights inside, reflects the architect's sensitivity toward potential residents as well as the planet.

↑ One configuration of the house includes a small courtyard with a fountain or pool. Above the siding, which can be made of either galvanized aluminum or COR-TEN steel, are operable clerestory windows.

← The master bedroom features louvered panels that can offer shade or, as shown, slide out of sight on a frame when more sun, or air, is desired.

↑ The interior features a loft-like space combining living room, dining room, and kitchen. The tall, narrow room is easily ventilated by cross-breezes flowing from sliding doors on the south side to clerestory windows on the north.

→ The kitchen features composite concrete countertops that include a high percentage of recycled material. The storage bar is finished with birch siding, and the flooring is made of bamboo.

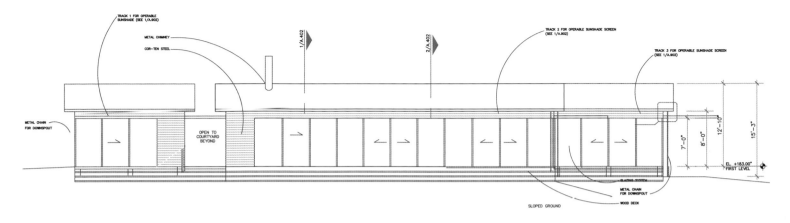

1/A.402
2/A.402

TRACK 1 FOR OPERABLE
SUNSHADE (SEE 1/A.902)

METAL CHIMNEY

COR-TEN STEEL

TRACK 2 FOR OPERABLE SUNSHADE SCREEN
(SEE 1/A.902)

TRACK 3 FOR OPERABLE SUNSHADE SCREEN
(SEE 1/A.902)

METAL CHAIN
FOR DOWNSPOUT

OPEN TO
COURTYARD
BEYOND

GLAZING SYSTEM

METAL CHAIN
FOR DOWNSPOUT

WOOD DECK

SLOPED GROUND

7'-0"

8'-0"

12'-10"

15'-3"

EL +183.00"
FIRST LEVEL

South Elevation

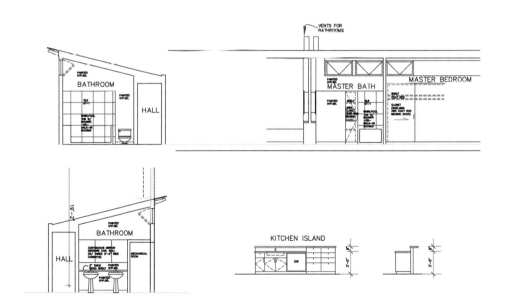

VENTS FOR
BATHROOMS

PAINTED
GYP. BD.

BATHROOM

PAINTED
GYP. BD.

HALL

TILE
SET-1

WHIRLPOOL
TUB W/
SHOWER

WALK-IN
SHOWER

PAINTED
GYP. BD.

MASTER BATH

MASTER BEDROOM

SHELF
(SHELVING
BEHIND)

LINEN
CLOSET
(SHELVING
BEHIND)

TILE
SET-1

WHIRLPOOL
TUB W/
SHOWER

WALK-IN
SHOWER

SHELF
COAT ROD

CLOSET
(SHELVING
AND COAT ROD
BEHIND DOOR)

19'-2"

PAINTED
GYP. BD.

BATHROOM

HALL

CONTINUOUS MIRROR
MEDICINE CAB. WALL
(W/ THREE 2'-6" WIDE
CABINETS)

1" THICK
WOOD SHELF

PAINTED
GYP. BD.

PAINTED
GYP. BD.

MECHANICAL
ROOM

KITCHEN ISLAND

DW

3'-0"

3'-0"

Section

← Section shows the double-
pitch of the multi-unit roofline.
The roof is angled for optimum
performance of (optional) solar
panels.

FEATURED ARCHITECTS

Joachim and Gabriele Achenbach
Achenbach Architekten + Designer
Reutlinger Strasse 93
Stuttgart D-70597
Germany
www.achenbach-architekten.com

Will Bruder
Will Bruder Architects
111 West Monroe, Suite 444
Phoenix, Arizona 85003
U.S.A.
www.willbruder.com

Cath Hall, Mike Verdouw, Fred Ward
1 + 2 Architecture
31 Melville Street
Hobart, Tasmania 7000
Australia
www.1plus2architecture.com

David Arkin and Anni Tilt
Arkin Tilt Architects
1101 8th Street, #180
Berkeley, California 94710
U.S.A.
www.arkintilt.com

Peter Carmichael
Cocks Carmichael
200 Gladstone Street
South Melbourne 3205
New South Wales
Australia

Frank Harmon
Frank Harmon and Associates
706 Mountford Street
Raleigh, North Carolina 27603
U.S.A.
www.frankharmon.com

Shigeru Ban
Shigeru Ban Architects
5-2-4 Matsubara, Setagaya-ku
Tokyo 156-0043
Japan
www.shigeruban.com

Georg Driendl
Driendl Architects
Mariahilferstrasse 9
A-1060 Vienna
Austria
www.driendl.at

David Hertz
David Hertz Architects/Syndesis
2908 Colorado Avenue
Santa Monica, California 90403
U.S.A.
www.syndesisinc.com

Mikko Bonsdorff
Arkkitehtitoimisto Okulus Oy
Kuortaneenkatu 5
00520 Helsinki
Finland

Allison Ewing and William McDonough
William McDonough + Partners
700 East Jefferson Street
Charlottesville, Virginia 22902
U.S.A.
www.mcdonoughpartners.com

Steven Holl
Steven Holl Architects
450 West 31st Street, 11th floor
New York, New York 10001
U.S.A.
www.stevenholl.com

Angela Brooks
Pugh + Scarpa Architecture
2525 Michigan Avenue, Building F1
Santa Monica, California 90404
U.S.A.
www.pugh-scarpa.com

Ted Flato, Bob Harris, Heather DeGrella
Lake/Flato Architects
311 Third Street, #200
San Antonio, Texas 78205
U.S.A.
www.lakeflato.com

Reijo Jallinoja
Arkkitehti Oy Reijo Jallinoja
Siltatie 1
00140 Helsinki
Finland

Rick Joy
Rick Joy Architects
400 South Rubio Avenue
Tucson, Arizona 85701
U.S.A.

Michelle Kaufmann
Michelle Kaufmann Designs
Novato, CA 94945
U.S.A.
www.michellekaufmanndesigns.com
www.glidehouse.com

Hannu Kiiskilä
ARRAK Arkkitchdit
Unioninkatu 45 B 42
00170 Helsinki
Finland
www.arrak.com

Rien Korteknie and Mechthild Stuhlmacher
Korteknie Stuhlmacher Architecten
's Gravendijkwal 73f
3021 EE Rotterdam
postbus 25012
3001 HA Rotterdam
The Netherlands
www.kortekniestuhlmacher.nl

Kengo Kuma
Kengo Kuma & Associates
2- 24- 8 Minami Aoyama
Minato- ku
Tokyo 107- 0062
Japan
www02.so-net.ne.jp/~kuma

Annabel Lahz and Andrew Nimmo
Lahz Nimmo Architects
Level 5
116 122 Kippax Street
Surry Hills, New South Wales 2010
Australia
www.lahznimmo.com

Brian MacKay-Lyons
Brian MacKay-Lyons Architects
2188 Gottingen Street
Halifax, Nova Scotia B3K 3B4
Canada
www.bmlaud.ca

Marsha Maytum and Roberto Sheinberg
Leddy Maytum Stacy Architects
677 Harrison Street
San Francisco, California 94107
U.S.A.
www.lmsarch.com

Dave Miller
The Miller/Hull Partnership
Polson Building
71 Columbia, 6th floor
Seattle, Washington 98104
U.S.A.
www.millerhull.com

Jim Olson
Olson Sundberg Kundig Allen Architects
159 South Jackson Street, 6th floor
Seattle, Washinton 98104
U.S.A.
www.olsonsundberg.com

Rafael Pelli
Cesar Pelli & Associates Architects
322 8th Avenue, 18th floor
New York, New York 10001
U.S.A.
www.cesar-pelli.com

Dietrich Schwarz
Schwarz Architektur
Via Calundis 8
CH-7013 Domat/Ems
Switzerland
www.schwarz-architektur.ch

Jennifer Siegal
Office of Mobile Design
1725 Abbot Kinney Boulevard
Venice, California 90291
U.S.A.
www.designmobile.com

Kirsti Siven
Kirsti Sivén & Asko Takala
Korkeavuorenkatu 25 A 5
00130 Helsinki
Finland

Werner Sobek
Werner Sobek Ingenieure
Albstrasse 14
70597 Stuttgart
Germany
www.wernersobek.com

RESOURCES

Alliance to
Save Energy
(www.ase.org)

Energy and Environmental
Building Association
(www.eeba.org)

Energy Star
Appliances Program
(www.energystar.gov)

Environmental
Building News
(www.buildinggreen.com)

Global Environmental
Options
(www.geonetwork.org)

Global Green
USA
(www.globalgreen.org)

Green Building
Alliance
(www.gbapgh.org)

Rocky Mountain
Institute
(www.rmi.org)

Sustainable
Building Industry Council
(www.sbicouncil.org)

U.S. Department
of Energy
(www.energy.gov)

U.S. Green
Building Council
(www.usgbc.org)

World Green Building
Council
(www.worldgbc.org)

PHOTOGRAPHY CREDITS

P.A.R.A.S.I.T.E.	Anne Bousema
156 Reade Street	Paul Warchol
Colorado Court	Marvin Rand
Viikki	Jussi Tiainen
130 East Union Street	James F. Housel/Benjamin Benschneider (p. 40 bottom left)
Sea Train House	Undine Pröhl
The Solaire	Jeff Goldberg/Esto
Solar Tube	Bruno Klomfar (p. 59 bottom)/James Morris
Charlotte Residence	Philip Beaurline
Villa Sari	Matti Karjanoja
Little Tesseract	Bilyana Dimitrova
Mill Valley Straw-Bale House	Edward Caldwell (p. 80; 83 top and middle)/John Dolan (p. 82; 83 bottom)
Naked House	Hirooyuki Hirai
House with Shades	Holger Hill
SolarHaus III	Frederic Comtesse
Great (Bamboo) Wall	Satoshi Asakawa
R128	Roland Halbe
Howard House	Undine Pröhl (p. 114; p. 117 left; p. 118 top left and right)
	James Steeves (p. 116; p. 117 right; p. 118 bottom left and right)
Swart Residence	Derek Swalwell
Lake Washington House	Eduardo Calderón
Walla Womba Guest House	1 + 2 Architecture/Peter Hyatt (p. 130)
McKinley House	Mark Seelen
Tucson Mountain House	Undine Pröhl
Giles Loft/Studio	Paul Hester
LoLoma 5 Lofts	Bill Timmerman
Casaurina Beach House	Brett Boardman
Taylor House	James West
Casa de Carmen	Luis Gordoa

This book is printed on NEO FSC matte,
an elemental chlorine free and acid free
paper.

The typefaces used in this book are
Thesis Serif, Clarendon, and
Rosewood.